The Art of
STRATEGIC
LEADERSHIP

The Art of

STRATEGIC

LEADERSHIP

How Leaders at All Levels Prepare Themselves, Their Teams, and Organizations for the Future

STEVEN J. STOWELL, Ph.D. AND STEPHANIE S. MEAD, MBA

WILEY

Contents

Acknowledgments vii

Preface ix

What You'll Find in This Book x

How to Use This Book xi

Chapter 1 Introduction 1

So, What Is It? 4

Why Does It Matter? 5

How You Can Use It 9

Chapter 2 The Business 11

Chapter 3 The Leader 19

Chapter 4 The Team 29

Chapter 5 Alex's Journey Begins 37

Chapter 6 The Art of Ownership 45

The Story: Robert 47

Ownership Close-Up 53

Chapter 7 The Art of Tenacity 63

The Story: Mya 65

	Tenacity Close-Up	70
	The Tenacity Formula	75
	Mastering Tenacity	78
Chapter 8	The Art of Risk	79
	The Story: Jordan	81
	Risk Close-Up	87
	Stepping Up	94
	A Note About Failure	96
Chapter 9	The Art of Agility	99
	The Story: Kim	101
	Agility Close-Up	105
	Your Flex-Agility	114
Chapter 10	The Art of Awareness	117
	The Story: Lu	119
	Awareness Close-Up	124
	What It All Means	130
Chapter 11	The Art of Driving Change	133
	The Story: Sara	135
	Driving Change Close-Up	140
Chapter 12	The Art of Vision	149
	The Story: Alex	151
	Vision Close-Up	156
	What Visionary Leaders Do	160
Chapter 13	The Art of Strategic Leadership	165
	The Rest of the Story	167
	The Future Starts Here and Now	176
Connect and Continue the Journey		*181*
About the Authors		*183*
Products and Services Available		*185*
Index		*187*

Acknowledgments

J ust like strategy, writing a book takes a team of people who catch the vision, believe in the idea, and know what winning means. We express our heartfelt gratitude to those individuals who took ownership for this project and worked tenaciously and collaboratively to help us articulate this important message. We genuinely believe it will make a difference to people working in organizations around the world. We want to especially thank Emily Hodgson–Soule and Howard Cohn for playing integral roles in this work. Your talents truly helped make this book possible. We also extend our sincere appreciation to Chris Stowell, Cyndi Keller, Debbie Stowell, Michelle Aamodt, and the entire CMOE team for working alongside us throughout this journey. And to our many clients who have allowed us to be their trusted partner over the years, we thank you, too. We couldn't have done any of this without you.

To our team of colleagues who helped interview, gather data, and work alongside strategic leaders in the field all over the world, this book represents the tremendous knowledge and insight you share with us every day: Eric Mead, Steve Nielsen, Bryan Yager, Rick Williams, Polly Scott, Tony Herrera, James Gehrke, Doug Trainor, and Dave Knapp.

And last but not least, words cannot express our thanks to you, our readers, for choosing to read this book and taking an interest in the art of strategic leadership.

Preface

It doesn't matter what position you hold in the organization—senior leader, mid-level manager, front-line manager, or leader of a group—your organization needs and wants you to be a strategic leader. When it comes to excelling as a leader, you cannot afford to stay in a strategic cocoon, insulated from a turbulent business environment, and neglect your responsibilities to think and act ahead of the curve. Markets, rivals, and the business environment all change too fast, are too complex, and are too competitive on a global scale for you not to be looking forward and leading your part of the business in a proactive way. Whether you lead sales, IT, quality, or another function in the business, you need to have a strong sense of direction, be aware of your strategic qualities, and have a deep concern for the future.

Leadership today is about more than just being operationally effective, solving existing problems, and guiding people through the normal work that needs to be done each day. Leadership is all about effectively executing short-term responsibilities while also shaping the future. The promise of a better future is what gets team members engaged and unleashes their motivation. When people are invited to be part of creating the future and can clearly see how they fit and why they matter, it causes them to do their best work.

In these challenging and exciting times, organizations desperately need leaders—at all levels—who have a vision and a plan to help move their teams to a better place and contribute value to the organization in new and unexpected ways.

What You'll Find in This Book

In our other books on strategic leadership and applied strategic thinking, we introduced processes, steps, and the how to's of creating strategy for your piece of the business. In this book, we chose to look at another facet of strategic leadership: the personal attributes that strategic leaders possess. We made this choice because our research indicates that leaders are hungry to know the unique leadership qualities that are necessary to be a driver and shaper of the future. Leaders need these qualities to fulfill the expectations that their organizations have of them. We've discovered that too often, people aren't clear on what these leadership attributes are or what they look like. This book responds to that compelling and broad-based need. We will help you look at strategy not from a process-oriented or tool-based perspective, but from the inside out. All leaders must possess and use these core qualities in order to lead and transform their teams and organizations for long-term, sustained growth.

Many works on leadership refer to the need for organizations to build their strategic-leadership bench strength at all levels of the business, but they don't thoroughly investigate and define how strategic leaders think, feel, and act as they set direction and execute on strategic goals and targets. We fill that void in two ways:

1. By exploring the qualities and values that enable strategic leaders to look out, look up, and look around.
2. Getting to the heart of what great strategic leaders actually *do* and the inner characteristics that drive them to be proactive.

We know that strategy formulation requires a clearly defined vision, long-term goals, useful tools, and a plan to win. But without the guidance of an insightful leader who can drive the process, it is difficult to make any strategy a reality. Ultimately, strategic leadership is what makes the difference between success or failure.

This book doesn't contain everything you need to know about strategy. It isn't intended to provide you with all there is to know about leadership, either. Instead, it provides a clear picture and makes you more conscious of the unique qualities and characteristics that will help you become a better leader and an active contributor to the long-term success of your organization. We've studied strategic thinking and leadership for a long time, and we've put our research and background to work for you. Our experience working closely with many different kinds of companies in a diverse variety of industries has allowed us to observe, study, and collaborate with all types of leaders as they apply strategy principles, build forward-thinking cultures, and execute long-term priorities in their businesses. As a result, we are able to share a framework for understanding the fundamental human qualities and characteristics of leaders who stand apart from the pack because they aren't just leaders—they're *strategic* leaders.

How to Use This Book

As you explore the ideas and concepts presented in these pages, we challenge you to reflect on your inner leadership core and capacity. See if there are opportunities to nurture the inherent qualities of strategic leadership and further your development in these areas—and then watch as your future unfolds. Taking ownership of the future is exciting work, especially when you start to see real results. We think you will be pleased with the outcomes of your efforts. Our hope is that as you read and study the concepts, you will find a few ideas that you can take away and apply immediately. We truly want you to be able to take advantage of the full spectrum of your potential and growth as a leader.

Choosing to read this book is a great first step down the path of developing greater strategic-leadership talent and capability. Strategic leadership doesn't need to be complicated. Don't think of it as one more thing to do. Instead, think of leading your teams as adding an additional layer of depth to your leadership style. Look for some insights about the qualities that you can develop and simply incorporate them into your current activities, knowledge, and abilities. Just imagine the impact you could have on your career, your organization, and the people around you if you were even the tiniest bit more strategic. If you are tired of being controlled by circumstances and would rather make a difference and actively shape the future, you've come to the right place—just start. The future begins now.

The Art of Strategic Leadership

1 | Introduction

You can't have strategy without leadership. They are inseparable. Sure, you can create a sound strategic plan, but to do something meaningful with it requires bold leadership. Having a great vision and setting a clear direction for the team lies at the very heart of leadership, and organizations that are filled with leaders who think and act strategically will be more successful than businesses with precious few leaders of this type—there's just no question about it.

So much value is lost for customers, owners, and employees when leaders fail to prepare for the future and take a role in actively shaping it. In our training, coaching, and consulting practice, we see a lot of leaders who are pretty good. But many of these leaders are so consumed by meeting the day-to-day demands of their businesses that they miss opportunities and overlook threats that are on the horizon. When we work inside organizations and coach leaders to become more proactive, we often run into managers who have good intentions but are consistently pulled back into a reactionary, problem-solving mode. No matter what they do, they can't seem to escape this vicious cycle and get ahead of the curve. We like how Warren Bennis describes it in *Why Leaders Can't Lead*: "Routine work drives out non-routine work and smothers to death all creative planning" (1989, p. 15). In *The Leadership Challenge*, Kouzes and Posner build on this idea by saying that the critical issue for leaders isn't whether they should have routines, but which routines they should have. The interesting thing is that some of the fires and problems consuming these leaders likely would have been averted completely—or at least managed more effectively—if they had used a little bit of foresight. Think about it. How many times have you heard leaders, even great ones, say, "If I had just thought ahead," or "Wow, that really caught me off guard," or "I just didn't see that opportunity coming," or "If only I had anticipated that, I could have been more proactive."

So, What Is It?

At this point, you may be wondering what, exactly, strategic leadership is. In our view, strategic leadership is a solution to the common leadership problems we just described. It's encompassed by two main things:

1. Fulfilling your regular leadership responsibilities in a proactive, forward-thinking way.
2. Incorporating a specific collection of qualities and characteristics into your leadership style as you lead your team and execute strategic objectives and plans.

There are only a few differences between normal, day-to-day leadership and strategic leadership, but they are big, and they are distinctive. The differences we've discovered all center around the way leadership principles are applied. Not only are strategic leaders concerned about fulfilling today's expectations, they also care deeply about defining and focusing on a future agenda that hones in on the few things that really matter. Defining a long-term vision for your team helps you allocate scarce resources wisely and channel the collective effort of the team. This prepares you to seize opportunities, head off threats, and achieve better results down the road. Remember, thinking, planning, and acting strategically shouldn't ever be considered solely a responsibility of senior leadership. All leaders, at all levels, are responsible for envisioning what they want in the future. They help their team members see the long-term vision clearly and create a plan for what we call their Business-within-the-Business. They do this by finding ways to create and leverage new sources of competitive advantage and unique, value-added offerings for their customers.

Why Does It Matter?

Why should you be a strategic leader? The reasons are pretty simple, actually. We have worked with numerous organizations around the world that need to elevate the performance of their leaders in order to maintain competitive advantage. Most use a leadership-competency model to clarify key leadership expectations. Over the years, we have noticed a shift in the requirements organizations have for their leaders in terms of their competencies. The evolution of these expectations and requirements is driven by many things, including technology, markets, competitors, social and economic variables, and the extraordinary quantity of changes facing organizations. This doesn't mean that what you've learned about leadership in the past no longer applies. What it does mean is that there are some fresh, new ideas that need to be considered and incorporated into your current understanding of effective leadership. This allows you to use and build on what you already know about leadership, but also broadens the notion of what makes a leader great in leading-edge organizations. In order to stay competitive, organizations need to be adaptive, creative, and move at an accelerated pace. What this means is that leadership as a practice must change, too.

One of the most-significant changes we have seen is that organizations now expect their leaders to be much more forward-thinking and proactive than they ever have before. We've also observed that there are a handful of important characteristics that differentiate strategic leaders from leaders of other types. In fact, nearly all of our clients have a leadership-competency model with a dimension that addresses the ability to think and act strategically. Just take a look at some of the examples below.

These revealing leadership expectations, which were taken from real organizations, leave no room for confusion about the necessity of strategic leadership today.

Sample Leadership–Competency Models

Organization 1

Thinks and acts strategically
- Sees the big picture
- Ensures alignment with overall strategies
- Understands long-term priorities
- Recognizes emerging patterns and trends
- Creates a compelling vision
- Courageously drives change
- Thinks creatively
- Is insightful and sees things from a new angle
- Is willing to experiment
- Anticipates customer needs

Organization 2

Leading growth: Makes strategic decisions
- Makes decisions to drive long-term success
- Considers the future in making decisions
- Translates strategy into practical steps for execution
- Uses strategy to set and explain priorities
- Seeks innovative ways to contribute to the growth of the business

Organization 3

Acts strategically
- Is future-focused and sees the big picture, business trends, and implications
- Is a source of fresh perspectives and challenges "the way it has always been done" objections

Organization 4

Thinks and acts strategically

- Thinks about future trends and consequences, which highlight opportunities to take action and shape the organization's future
- Seeks to understand the business's strategic direction
- Identifies and articulates a compelling strategy and strategic vision for the future
- Demonstrates a big-picture view of the business
- Anticipates future business trends accurately, and responds quickly and effectively
- Identifies new business processes that are key to future success

Clearly, many organizations feel the need to have more long-term, proactive thinking occurring among leaders at all levels of their businesses. From what we've seen, it's evident that most leaders work hard to make their teams and organizations better, but many are so focused on the short-term, day-to-day routines, and on fighting fires, that they neglect to work on long-term priorities. Our aim in this book is to familiarize you with the fundamental characteristics and qualities that are necessary for you to be successful with the strategic-leadership expectations—explicit or not—that your organization has of you.

Knowing what it will take for you to win over the long haul and having goals and strategies to pursue is critically important—but that's not all that matters. Strategic leaders take it one step farther. They actively engage and leverage the organization's pool of talent not only to achieve short-term results, but to work *with* them to set a direction that will produce long-term results and create a secure and prosperous future for everyone.

Sometimes leaders have a hard time understanding why they can't get better traction with important changes that need to be made, critical business plans, or long-term initiatives. Remarkable effort goes into creating goals, plans, and strategies. Most of the time, the strategy or plans aren't the problem; it's the lack of strategic leadership that's the bottleneck. Simply put, the thing that is missing most often is the leadership necessary to translate strategic ideas into reality. Leaders must have the personal qualities and discipline necessary to push the implementation of these important priorities through to completion.

Everywhere we go there is an intense appetite for insights into the makeup of a proactive, strategic leader and how to develop those capabilities. People are grasping for practical solutions to these challenges. Business leaders want to know how to lead their teams strategically while keeping things practical and down to earth. Don't get us wrong: We know that high-level strategy matters, but so does integrating a strategic mindset into the heart of the organization and enrolling leaders at all levels in creating strategic plans for their parts of the business. That said, we also recognize that leaders can't work in a strategic mode all the time and that balancing the urgent demands of today with the important priorities that sustain long-term advancement is a daunting task. But what leaders can constantly do is look at everything they do through a proactive lens. That's the key. The qualities and underlying principles of strategic leadership need to act as your frame of reference. They will guide your pattern of leadership behaviors and thoughts, and those matter a lot when it comes to making a difference in the organization. People who have combined their leadership style with strategic ideas and plans are far more likely to achieve the results they desire because it is a person's fundamental behaviors and frame of mind that brings strategy, goals, and plans to life.

The future speeds toward us with greater velocity, more complexity, and greater uncertainty, but we still have a choice in how we respond to these challenges: We can either be driven by the forces of change or we can choose to be proactive and drive. Being a driver means taking some risks, running some experiments, anticipating and preparing for eventualities, and offering innovative solutions.

Strategy, at any level, seeks an answer to one basic question: How do you add value, introduce new services, and not just embrace best practices but actually invent the next practices that will ensure you remain relevant in your business environment?

The simple truth is that the future won't be any different from the way things are now if you and your team continue to do the same things in the same way. If the internal rate of change doesn't exceed the external rate of change, you will lose the race. To win, you and your organization need to anticipate what's coming and invest in the future now. Strategic leaders go to work every day—thinking, planning, and acting on challenges and opportunities that lie ahead—because they care about the future and know they can play an important role in creating it.

How You Can Use It

What makes strategic leaders stand out from the crowd? To illustrate their unique qualities, it's crucial to see them in action, so we will share with you the story of Alex, a bright leader about to tackle the greatest challenge of his career: charting an exciting new direction for his team in a highly competitive industry. As he interacts with his six department heads, you will observe the inner workings of his mind and get acquainted with the core qualities and characteristics of strategic leadership up close and personal. Each member of Alex's team possesses a unique talent, and over time, Alex is able to harness these special competencies and guide his part of the business to a better place. The twists and turns, intrigue, and drama will pull you through, and you'll relate to the story's recognizable situations and characters.

The people and dilemmas you will read about are based on the practical, strategic challenges managers face in a demanding business environment. Following each narrative section of Alex's story, we discuss concepts and suggestions that are directly applicable to leaders seeking solutions in their quest for long-term success. As you'll discover, when the right mindset and approaches are combined with clear plans and strategic direction, the outcomes are remarkable.

Throughout this book, we will explore the seven essential qualities of strategic leaders, the attributes that have the greatest impact on setting a direction and helping the organization change. The sections analyzing those qualities will help you assess your own strategic-leadership strengths and areas that you'll want to cultivate. By using what you learn, developing new capabilities, and applying strategic approaches to your unique situation, you will be better prepared to respond to business challenges, leverage new opportunities, and excel in your role.

One final note: We have structured the book so it will reward two types of readers: those who read from the first chapter to the last and those who scan the contents and zero in on the aspects of strategic leadership they find most interesting, challenging, or urgent. We know your time is precious and we want to put it to good use.

Let's hit the road!

2 | The Business

Look around you. Think about the products that affect your quality of life. The contact lenses on your bathroom shelf. The molded bumpers on your car. The precision plastics that are integral parts of the airplanes we fly, the surgical devices we use, the medical implants we rely on, and the technological devices that keep us connected to the world around us. They're just a few of the countless advanced polymer- and composite-based products we use every day.

The role that composites and polymers play in our lives goes far beyond consumer convenience. As nations and corporations focus on reducing their environmental impacts, by saving energy and improving product performance, nearly every industry is racing to incorporate sustainable, lightweight, and durable materials into their products.

Polymer Solutions, Inc. (PSI), based in New Jersey, was founded in the 1980s by a group of chemists and engineers who did research and secured patents in the aerospace, electronics, and biotech industries. A privately held company, PSI branched out from its beginnings as a supplier of high-performance engineering plastics for defense and aerospace manufacturers, as well as medical and surgical applications. Highly regarded for design, engineering, and reliability, in recent years PSI expanded into markets in electronics, energy, the automotive and transportation sectors, telecommunications, and consumer products.

Much of the credit for the business's recent growth goes to Melissa, PSI's CEO. Trained as a chemist, Melissa, who also holds an MBA, joined the company as senior vice president for marketing and was promoted to CEO five years later. One of her first initiatives was the construction of a new state-of-the-art manufacturing facility on land adjacent to the outdated plant in New Jersey. With Seattle already operating at near-peak capacity and new orders for standard and custom products multiplying, Melissa spearheaded a plan to establish a physical presence in markets where PSI saw opportunities to expand its customer base.

PSI has amassed a sizeable war chest to spend on new facilities, and attracted the interest of several private-equity firms ready to invest in the company's expansion. In addition to doubling its manufacturing capacity, PSI intended to attract new customers and develop new products that make use of the latest polymer and composite materials and technologies.

Initially, Melissa and the board believed the most strategic location would be the Middle East, bringing PSI closer to petrochemical producers, or Asia, where the company was gaining market share in the region's fast-growing economies. That game plan changed when two U.S.-based plants—owned by another company and complete with their own product lines, customer bases, and engineering and operations staff—unexpectedly came on the market. The sites, in Chicago and Dallas, were the polymer-products division of a midsized firm that had decided to focus operations on their core metals business instead of polymers and composites. PSI sent a team led by Victor, the COO, to visit both plants; they returned with some bold but risky ideas. Victor saw their potential immediately. "Their product lines are a bit behind the times, and the physical plants will need serious upgrades if they're to become value-added members of the PSI family and compete in the future," Victor told Melissa on his return, "but the engineering and operations talent is good, especially when you consider their corporate management's been neglecting them for the past several years. They're hungry for new direction and new leadership."

Since the price was right for these assets, that was all Melissa and the board needed to hear to pull the trigger on the acquisition. Melissa is all about formulas. In her view, long-term success is less about cutting costs and more about recognizing investment opportunities and acting decisively. As soon as the deal was sealed, Melissa set to work scouring her in-house talent pool for potential plant managers for the two new plants.

Whenever Melissa fills a key position—department or team leader, plant manager, sometimes even an individual contributor whose role is critical—she demands three abilities or traits:

1. Delivery on short-term commitments and results.
2. Strong team values: collaboration, transparency, open communication.
3. A keen eye for the future: thinking long-term, seizing opportunities, closing the gap on personal strategic weak spots (Melissa's term is "the strategic Achilles heel").

No doubt these loomed large in her decision to put Alex in charge of the Dallas plant.

Alex jumped at the chance to run the show in Dallas. He held an engineering degree as well as an MBA and had joined PSI at the manager level. He caught Melissa's eye when he conducted a study employing management tools and techniques to improve quality in his department. As part of her effort to turn quality into a competitive advantage, she invited him to head a small task force that shared the study's conclusions and methodology with other business units. The report and subsequent process, called *Quality Without Borders*, was a great success across the company.

After that, Alex's reputation, qualities, and skills grew rapidly. Recently, however, although he'd completed PSI's 18-month Rising Leader development program, he didn't see an immediate opportunity for advancement. He and his current department head, the vice president of engineering, were close in age and experience, and the COO job held by Victor, his current boss, wasn't likely to come open for a long time. Dallas was an opportunity to make an end run around these obstacles and gain deep experience turning a plant around.

Alex concurred with Victor's recommendation to retain the staffs at both of the newly acquired plants. Only he and his counterpart in Chicago, the other plant manager, would be transplanted from PSI. Alex shared his observations with Victor on the flight back from their second Dallas visit, saying, "There's bound to be some attrition, but if we bring in too many people from the mother ship, they'll think we don't believe they'll be able to come up to our standards and meet our expectations. And I think they can."

"Besides," Victor said wryly, "think of what will happen to Seattle if we cannibalize their best talent and send them to Dallas."

Still, Alex knew it wasn't going to be easy. Some of the employees were demoralized, and for good reason: The former owners had held off on investing in the plant and allowed it to stumble along while they waited for the right moment to unload it. The competition in the region was also heating up; in recent months, one competitor had opened up a new plant in Houston, and others might be in the works. A fully air-conditioned facility that offered superior safety features might entice even dedicated workers to jump ship—especially those struggling to work in an aging plant. Additionally, a less-than-sterling record for on-time delivery and questionable product quality were obstacles—to the plant's survival, let alone its long-term success—that Alex needed to do something about in a hurry.

PSI made earlier acquisitions but, until now, that always meant moving people and products to the existing facilities. This time, PSI was proposing to export a part of itself—its values and vision, a trickier challenge than transferring physical equipment or processes—to Chicago and Dallas. The senior leadership team anticipated that bringing the plants and personnel up to PSI standards and making them full members of the PSI family would take three years, possibly longer. Alex wondered if that would be enough time to transform Dallas.

Alex also suspected that Dallas and Chicago may be at the starting line of a competition over which plant will still be part of PSI in three years. In fact, it's Melissa's little secret that PSI intended to add only one American production site until the Chicago-Dallas package deal came along. Senior management, the board, and the investors who made the purchase possible were planning to retain the better-performing operation at the end of three years and sell, shutter, or relocate the mediocre plant to Mexico or Puerto Rico.

Alex wasn't overly concerned. He knew there would be a job for him back in Seattle—or even at the home office in New Jersey—if Dallas didn't pan out, but that wasn't the reason. He was confident, passionate, and determined to succeed in Dallas; to paraphrase Melissa, he saw his chance and was poised to make the most of this once-in-a-lifetime opportunity. He liked the location, especially since it included a lease on fifteen acres of land adjacent to the existing plant, with an option to purchase, should PSI decide its roots in Dallas were permanent. Interstate 45 also offered a cheap and convenient transportation link to the raw-materials supply chain in Houston, the petrochemical hub, and its port. This location gave Dallas a huge natural competitive advantage in terms of transportation costs.

Alex conceded that the Chicago plant had enjoyed longer relationships with its Midwestern customers—particularly auto-makers and equipment manufacturers—and with some companies that produced medical equipment. But because both are industries with growing presences in the southern states and in Mexico, Alex felt that he might even succeed in stealing market share from Chicago in those areas. His chief edge, he was certain, was the quality of the people he had met when he visited the plant, from department leaders to shift workers. They were ready for an inspired leader and a new direction; they'd be open to the strategic transformation needed to guarantee Dallas's future as an essential part of PSI. Alex knew that it would take good people to make his agenda a reality, and with the right leadership, they'd be equal to the challenges of complex customer requirements, new product materials and production, and unforgiving schedules. Alex was ready to instill that culture, work with his team to solve the plant's short-term problems, and develop a plan to capture market share and upgrade the plant's capacity and quality through increased automation over the coming three to five years.

3 | The Leader

Alex wasn't surprised when Melissa told him the Dallas plant manager position was his. He was the only mid-level manager invited to join Victor for their due-diligence, prepurchase evaluations of both new sites, so Alex knew he was very much in the running for the job. No, what surprised him was that almost at the same moment as the sense of euphoria engulfed him, he found himself thinking, *What have I gotten into?* His excitement at the long-awaited opportunity returned in a flash, and he was confident that Melissa hadn't noticed any hint of his fleeting failure of confidence. He accepted the offer on the spot.

For months, Alex and his wife Julie had been talking about the possibility of leaving Seattle, ever since he'd woken up to the fact that if he remained there, it might be years before a chance to take on more responsibility materialized. Until recently, his progress at PSI had been swift, but that was due to his success with a number of special projects and assignments, like the *Quality Without Borders* initiative that had put him on Melissa's radar in the first place. Since then, he'd enjoyed similar successes with other special projects, but they hadn't opened any doors to new career opportunities and challenges. At length, Alex realized that although he was advancing the corporation's strategic goals, he was largely neglecting his own aspirations.

As he walked back to his office, he left a brief message for Julie: "Start packing!" though they wouldn't actually be moving households for another few months. It was early May; their two boys, ages 6 and 11, were still in school; and Julie, a high school science teacher, wouldn't wrap up her academic year until late June. But at home that evening, she was more excited than Alex. "It's a perfect time to start fresh," she told him. "Sam will be going into second grade, Michael will be starting middle school, and I'll apply for a leave of absence from the school, just in case it doesn't work out. While you're learning the ropes in Dallas, I'll hold down the fort here. The boys will be in camp most of the summer, so I'll have plenty of time to find a family to rent our house for a year."

"Are you sure you won't regret leaving your teaching career, our friends, everything we've built here?" Alex asked.

"It's the challenge you've been waiting for, and I'm ready to try life in a new part of the country, especially one where it doesn't rain four days out of seven."

That settled it, and a week later, after promising to spend at least every other weekend with Julie and their boys, Alex was making himself at home in his new office in the Dallas plant. While driving down from Seattle with everything he would need for the two months of bachelor existence in Texas, he'd created a mental map for transforming PSI's troubled new acquisition into a model for the future.

He envisioned the transition as unfolding in three stages. During Phase One, lasting eight weeks, he would familiarize himself with everything that went on at the Dallas plant and get to know everyone who contributed to it, especially the six team leaders who reported directly to him. He needed to understand them and their talents, and really assess what they would bring to the table.

Phase Two would focus on immediate operational problems, so-called fix-and-prune issues, that could be addressed in the 12-month window Alex projected for this stage in Dallas's evolution. It was too soon to earmark specific initiatives, but he and Victor had discussed a number of possibilities when they analyzed the plant's history: friction between Operations and Quality Control that dragged productivity down, turnover issues and operator training, and too-frequent problems with the handoffs between engineering and production. Since these and other possible short-term challenges involved cooperation between departments, Alex expected plenty of resistance—and maybe even finger-pointing. That didn't deter him. In fact, he planned to turn these opportunities into pilot projects aimed at fostering a culture of collaboration in Dallas.

Phase Three, developing a long-term blueprint for the Dallas plant's future and aligning it with PSI's mission, would grow organically out of the early wins that he'd secure. That part would be big, bold, fun—and risky. Its chances of success would depend on a number of factors:

- How well the short-term improvements worked out.
- How effectively Alex integrated the principles of strategic leadership into the plant's culture, and especially among his core group of team leaders.
- Whether Alex can persuade senior management from the home office, PSI's board, and its cadre of investors to believe in the vision and commit new capital.

To enable Dallas to play a key role in PSI's next generation, it needed a new, state-of-the-art plant capable of matching its competitors in technology, one that could even be capable of supporting R&D projects. That future is perhaps five years out, though Alex hoped to bring it to fruition sooner. He called his vision The Plan.

Alex had good reason for being in a hurry to make the case for Dallas's future prospects: He was fairly certain that one of the two newly acquired plants wouldn't be around for long. Until the former owners put these two plants on the market as a package, the talk in the home office was about acquiring or building just one additional manufacturing facility. In fact, on the flight back from their final inspection of the Dallas plant, Victor, thinking out loud, had said, "A week ago, we were looking for one plant. A week from now, we'll double that." Since then, no one—and certainly not Melissa or Victor—had said anything explicit about pitting the two locations against one another, and nothing at all had been said about one of the facilities being in jeopardy, but Alex knew both Melissa and Victor well enough to read between the lines: Get results early and show that your vision of the future works or you won't have a plant to manage for long.

During his first week in Dallas, however, Alex was far too busy keeping up with the day-to-day life of the plant to brood about what might happen a year—or even three years—from now. He'd spent more than half his working life in the industry, so the physical layout and operations of the plant were familiar to him, though some of the technology and equipment were so antiquated he sometimes had to remind himself that he wasn't in an industrial museum. More importantly, he needed to get to know the entire staff, and he was determined to make himself a familiar, approachable presence to every employee—even those who worked the overnight shift, a group that sometimes felt invisible. Temporarily freed from domestic routine, Alex could arrive at work early or late, drop in at odd hours to chat with front-line workers on their breaks, and casually take note of how members of different departments interacted; whether, for example, Maintenance and Operations collaborated to keep the often-problematic equipment running as efficiently as possible, and how frequently team leaders communicated with their direct reports and with each other.

Friendly, unceremonious, curious, and a good listener, Alex quickly became a welcome presence everywhere he went. He has a knack for observing people at their jobs without making them feel like they were under surveillance and for asking questions that were born out of sheer curiosity, not a test of the employee's knowledge or competence. Alex started spending an entire week's worth of afternoons with each of the plant's team leaders. Before two weeks had passed, nearly everyone felt at ease in his presence. He watched, listened, and occasionally asked a question or offered a suggestion, but he never overruled a team leader or pulled rank with the workers.

As a result, Alex absorbed the plant's current processes and systems in depth and paid close attention to the personal styles of his team of managers, as well as how they interacted with members of their own departments and the rest of the Dallas staff. He was fascinated by how different the six were from one another: Jordan, the head of engineering; Robert, the operations chief; Mya, who ran the quality group; Lu, the leader of the maintenance team; Kim, in human resources; and Sara, finance and supply chain leader (see Figure 3.1).

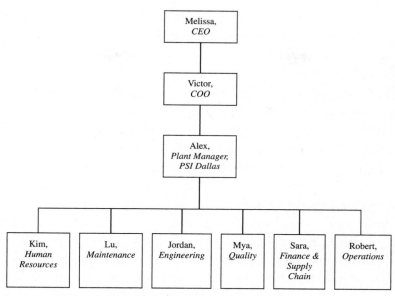

Figure 3.1   PSI Leadership Team

In each department leader, Alex noticed decided gifts and talents that he believed could contribute to their collective future— for example, how Robert's deep knowledge of the plant and attention to detail kept Operations on its toes—while at the same time, noticing where their weaknesses lay—as when Mya held up the line when she thought too many products had fallen out of spec. Observing them over many hours, discussing their work and how they expected things to change, Alex got to know their management styles and how much they thought about what the future held for the industry and Dallas's place in that future. At times, some of them didn't seem to be thinking about that enough, or even at all. However, even at this early stage, Alex sensed something of value in each of them, though it was hard for him to specifically pinpoint the unique characteristics and potential talents that each person could offer.

They might be a mixed bag, Alex decided, but they certainly deserved credit for keeping the Dallas plant on its feet in spite of the previous owners' years of neglect, lack of vision, and other leadership shortcomings. Alex learned from his team that once the company decided to get out of polymer manufacturing, management had stopped upgrading technology, cut corners on maintenance, and chose the lowest-cost (and therefore, lowest-quality) suppliers. It came as no surprise that the plant's reputation suffered and some customers took their business elsewhere as a result. What impressed Alex was that the employees managed to keep their rudderless ship afloat. Now, with PSI in charge, they had reason to hope for a much brighter future. Alex planned to raise their sights quite a bit higher. What was needed now was fresh vision, a strong dose of leadership, and a strategy that would produce a win–win for PSI, future customers, and—especially—the employees who would make it happen.

To give his ideas concrete form for the team leaders, Alex shared a simple diagram with them, shown in Figure 3.2, that embodied his vision in a nutshell.

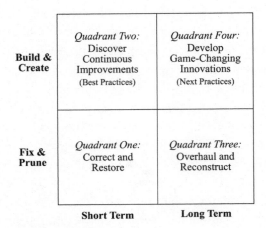

Figure 3.2　Alex's Vision

Alex was confident that his leadership and energy could bring about the short-term gains that would make management receptive to his business case for committing to an ambitious transformation in Dallas. Alex's goal was to upgrade the existing facility and eventually add new capacity to accommodate new customers on the adjacent property. That would give Dallas a shot at being an innovative leader in the industry in process manufacturing, engineering, and development. If necessary, he'd settle for rebuilding from the ground up, but that wasn't his ultimate plan.

Alex reminded himself that changing the team's mindset, getting them to see the status quo merely as a starting point, would be the toughest—and most crucial—step. He expected it would be an easy sell to persuade them to adopt best practices to raise productivity and quality, improve safety, and reduce waste. But getting the plant back to where it should have been before Alex arrived, fixing today's problems—or worse, yesterday's—wouldn't be good enough. The team had to start looking ahead, creating *next* practices, to ensure that Dallas could keep pace with a rapidly evolving business environment. Otherwise, the plant wouldn't make it: Customers would turn to the competition, and the home office in New Jersey would write Dallas off. Alex was determined to retain Dallas's current customers, woo back old ones, and win new ones. Nothing less would sell PSI management on Dallas's place in the company's future.

4 | The Team

During his first week or two in Dallas, Alex marveled at how different his department leaders were from one another. Despite—or perhaps because of—their contrasting styles, they genuinely got along, and not merely in the cordial, but distant, manner of professional colleagues, but with honest curiosity and concern about their lives in and out of their work environment. Mya, who is from Brazil, and Robert, born and raised in the shadow of the old football stadium in Irving, Texas, sometimes butted heads over production-quality standards, but they teased each other like siblings about whether soccer or American football is the genuine article.

Among the others, Lu and Jordan disagreed almost daily about whether maintenance or engineering should claim responsibility when a customized product proved difficult to manufacture, but they chatted endlessly about their shared interest in the latest advances in technology and their love of tinkering with complex equipment and electronics.

Some team members were natural allies about workplace issues, but kept their distance in other ways. Kim, the head of HR, and Sara, the Dallas plant's financial guru, waged a vocal campaign to curb attrition, a costly drain on efficiency, morale, and the bottom line. They're even close in age and background. But someone who noticed them around the plant might assume they were strangers. Lively and upbeat, Kim's personality overshadowed that of Sara, whose reflective, analytical character tended to hide her steely confidence from anyone who wasn't paying very close attention.

To Alex, the team members' distinctive attributes and willingness to voice their disagreements were positive signs, hinting at the sort of creative tension he intended to encourage. Openness to other points of view, finding common ground, and looking for ways to benefit the whole plant (as well as its individual parts) are building blocks of the art of strategic leadership. Nevertheless, he realized that none of the team leaders had any inkling that Alex was already thinking in terms of a multi-year evolutionary path

31

for Dallas. Most of them—though probably not all—continued to believe that if they just did a better job of retaining skilled operators and upgraded a handful of obsolete equipment, they'd solve the bulk of the plant's productivity and quality problems, win their lost customers back, and be assured of a rosy future.

Alex didn't share his conviction that these steps and similar fix-and-prune opportunities were, at best, only the first steps toward stabilizing the plant's operation and securing its future. By themselves, they wouldn't accomplish nearly enough to save the plant, but Alex read them as signs of a readiness to do what it takes, and he intended to build on them. But for the moment, he was still figuring out what worked and what didn't and observing the subtle dynamics of his leadership team's interactions as a group. He'd begun to notice who was likely to propose new initiatives that demanded cross-departmental cooperation, who usually signed on or at least offered moral support for the transformation, and who hung back or, sometimes, resisted change.

If the relatively limited fix-and-prune initiatives can be compared to day trips along well-marked highways, launching a three- to five-year strategic plan resembles a sea voyage across uncharted waters, but with one crucial difference: The captain and crew are continuing to build their ship as they struggle to sail toward their destination, which they cannot yet see with perfect clarity and might never reach. Training his crewmembers to leverage their strategic talents, map out their long-range plans for Dallas, and execute them successfully will certainly have its share of risks. Some members of the team may think twice before signing on, but the enthusiasm they'd already shown suggested to Alex that they're game.

If there is one shortcoming nearly all the team members share, it's a tendency to take shelter behind the protective walls of their departmental silos, especially when crisis looms. Perhaps, Alex thought, this is a vestige of the survival tactics they adopted to shield themselves and their people from the harsh, cost-cutting measures that were implemented by the previous owners after they decided to unload the plants.

One incident that occurred a few weeks before Alex took over the reins in Dallas was a classic illustration of the syndrome. The manufacturing engineers and design engineers from corporate had developed a whole new concept for an instrument-control panel, a custom design for a large customer. The customer thought the design was even better than they had hoped, but when Operations had trouble manufacturing the item to meet the delivery and cost constraints, Jordan, head of engineering, hesitated before assigning engineers to help solve the production problems. Robert, the operations leader, finally forced the issue, but by then, delays and frequent rejects cut into the profitability of the project and the goodwill they'd built with the customer.

Alex learned of the episode from a veteran operator, Claire, who was one of the first employees he spoke to at length shortly after his arrival. Had Alex been on the scene when the crisis flared, he realized he would have stepped in despite his pledge to observe, not intervene until Phase One of The Plan ended.

A few less-dire instances occurred later as well. On one occasion, Maintenance, Lu's department, was slow to respond when some of the antiquated equipment wouldn't stay calibrated, holding up production. From time to time, his group also ignored potential safety hazards on the production floor—personal safety gear, faulty guards on equipment, chemical spills, and the like. And during the tense period when Operations was struggling with production of the customized control panel that caused them such headaches, Mya, the leader over quality, caused a minor scuffle when she insisted that a large number of the products were below quality standards. Sales and Engineering finally convinced her that this wasn't the case, but production was brought to a standstill while the calibration issue was checked and rechecked.

What was often absent from the leaders' outlook, Alex saw, was an enterprise mindset; acknowledgment that the butterfly effect is real: A minor disturbance at any stage in a process may lead to disastrous results at the end. In just his first few weeks, Alex heard too many "If only they . . ." statements from people who should have been thinking *How can I get us back on course and prevent similar breakdowns in the future?* The staff, from the team leaders on down, was loaded with talented, highly skilled operators, materials specialists, software engineers, supply-chain managers, mechanics, and accountants, despite the departure of a number of highly valued employees. But they needed to shift focus from their narrow specialties to the big picture if they were to contribute their full value to PSI.

For the moment, Alex welcomed the staff's unsolicited efforts to reverse the plant's slips in quality measures and key operational indicators that had damaged its reputation with customers and threatened profitability. Getting things back to where they were wouldn't mean that the plant was in good shape, however. Good may be better, but it was no longer good enough.

Alex knew this before he left Seattle; he had done his homework. The use of composites and polymer products in industry, high tech, and consumer applications is in continual flux. Seemingly overnight, customer requirements for new applications, designs, devices, and materials multiply and grow increasingly sophisticated, and any producer that fails to keep pace with this rapid evolution is left behind. PSI Dallas would need change agents: people who can plainly see what's coming. Others, focused solely on short-term efficiencies, are blind to these signals. PSI Dallas needed people to play a part in planning innovative strategies and raising the plant to the parent company's high standards—and perhaps even exceeding them. To grab the brass ring, Alex knew that Dallas would almost certainly have to outperform Chicago in both its day-to-day operations and through its long-term plan to win.

Alex had confidence in the team's ability to integrate a strategic outlook with their current leadership styles, and he was impatient to get started. He remembered Victor's assertion that the talent and potential of Dallas's leadership team was as good a reason for acquiring the plant as its infrastructure and existing business. Still, he planned to proceed cautiously. From experience, he knew that entrenched staffers can be skeptical of a new leader, let alone one with a lofty vision for the business. They needed time to get used to his management style—and to a new way of thinking. Until then, the quick wins that would result from Alex's short-term Phase Two initiatives would serve as test cases of how much—and unfortunately, how little—could be achieved by collaborating across departmental lines and tearing down silos. Alex expected that the team would conclude on its own that fixing and pruning alone won't save the plant. When they did, they'd be ready to start looking beyond the near horizon.

Over the weeks Alex spent closely observing his six department leaders, each of them revealed reservoirs of talent, openness to ideas, and dedication to the growth of PSI Dallas. Their very different personalities also complemented one another well: Robert's deep concern about the plant and the workers; Jordan's confidence and technical brilliance; Mya's meticulous attention to detail; Sara's knack for seeing the plant as a single, unified process; Lu's familiarity with every nut and bolt in the building, as well as the idiosyncrasies of the plant's equipment; and Kim's uncanny ability to find new solutions to really complex problems.

These traits and qualities, Alex knew, would help the team formulate a coherent, ambitious strategy for Dallas—and execute it. All Alex had to do was tease these talents out of each individual, infuse them into the team as a whole, and let them loose to turn the vision for Dallas into reality. He was ready to lay the groundwork.

5 | Alex's Journey Begins

For eight weeks, Alex explored every corner of the Dallas plant, observing operators working on the line, maintenance crews tending and repairing equipment, quality technicians testing products, engineers designing new processes, and warehouse workers inspecting incoming materials and packing finished items for shipment. He inspected equipment, talked to employees about conditions at the plant and their lives outside of work, and peered over the shoulders of the team leaders as they conducted business, interacted with their people, fielded questions, and responded to problems. He wanted to get to know the members of the Dallas community, observe them at work, and pinpoint the plant's current strengths and opportunities for improvement. The first step to shaping the future, Alex knew, was seeing clearly where things stood in the present.

Alex was pleasantly surprised by how readily people shared their views about where the plant needed to improve over the long haul, as well as what they thought it did well. One of Alex's first steps as manager was a town hall-type meeting with the entire staff. After introducing himself, he assured everyone that he hadn't come to Dallas to clean house; there were no plans to lay off workers or bring in new department heads. He was there to listen and learn and to leverage their knowledge and experience in charting a course for a secure future for the Dallas plant as a vital part of PSI.

As it turned out, there were no secrets in the Dallas plant. Throughout those early weeks, it seemed there were more days when something went wrong than days when something didn't. One of the more-dramatic incidents occurred about a month earlier, when the master circuit-breaker panel failed, cutting off power throughout the building. Everyone seemed genuinely surprised, except for Alex—and maybe Lu, head of maintenance. Alex had already seen that the plant, which was twenty years old and lacking a rigorous maintenance plan, was full of aging, obsolete equipment. It wasn't a question of if but when a critical component like the 1600-amp breaker would stop working.

While Lu and his key electricians assessed the damage, Alex heard more than a few people wisecracking that now they couldn't even charge their cellphones. This can't be such an uncommon occurrence after all, Alex thought.

In the past, he learned, the outages had been limited, and Lu had always been able to locate a replacement or cannibalize older equipment. This time, it was the entire system, and the manufacturer hadn't made that specific panel for five years. Lu finally found a new panel at a supplier in Ohio, but production was interrupted for a full day before it could be installed. Nearly two additional days passed before operations completely returned to normal. The resulting lag in production and late deliveries hurt the company's image with several key customers.

"We need to be attracting new customers, not losing old ones," muttered Robert, the operations manager. Silently, Alex agreed, but he didn't want to seem to be faulting Lu and his maintenance crew for the incident. He wasn't happy about the breakdown or the sorry state of the plant's infrastructure. But he realized that whenever something serious went wrong, it opened a window onto an area of the plant or a process that demanded a long-term vision.

There was no shortage of learning opportunities those first eight weeks. When three experienced operators abruptly resigned in one week, Operations had a hard time keeping production on schedule, and Kim, the HR manager, was hard-pressed to find replacements. Problems with the quality of an entire production run and minor damage to one of the machines also resulted in lost manufacturing time, as did a substandard shipment of raw materials that wasn't properly inspected when it was delivered to the plant.

The obvious lessons of these and similar events weren't lost on the staff: the plant needed a scheduled, preventive maintenance plan, incentives to retain good employees, better end-to-end quality controls, and improved safety practices. For his part, Alex appreciated how the physical deficiencies of the plant conspired to trap the staff in a nearly continuous crisis mode. But he also seized the

Figure 5.1   Strategy Engine

opportunity to heighten the team leaders' awareness of the damage that can be done to a business when its short-term operational and tactical elements are out of sync with its strategic plans and direction. As soon as the circuit-breaker crisis passed, he shared a diagram (see Figure 5.1) with them that he employed with great success in a program he implemented for PSI several years earlier.

When Alex walked through the diagram with the team, they reacted enthusiastically, and without finger-pointing. Although the power failure was the obvious example of a technical malfunction, all six team leaders admitted to comparable problems in their own areas. They also understood how the absence of any strategic plan—or even of discussions aimed at formulating one—increased the likelihood that a catastrophe would occur. It was like trying to steer a ship without a rudder.

In the discussion that followed, Alex stressed that it wasn't possible to eliminate risk entirely—and it wasn't a good idea to try.

"A plan with zero risk is also a plan with zero opportunity," he told the team. But if Dallas could anticipate—and ward off—some of the potential problems, it would be in a position to capitalize on opportunities that would arise. "Just think," he said, "PSI bought the Dallas plant when it came on the market because it saw how Dallas fit into the company's plans for its future, but could Dallas have responded quickly to a similar opportunity, or would it have been too busy treading water and fighting fires?"

Running a plant, he continued, is like putting a large, complex jigsaw puzzle together, except that the puzzle changes shape every day. In fact, it's like two related puzzles, a short-term game and a long-term game, that intersect at unpredictable and imperceptible points. With a strategically focused team, it's possible to hold things together, even as the puzzle changes from day to day. A nimble team manages to deal with the wild cards thrown at it, both those that are internal (power outages and manufacturing snafus) and those that are external (supplier problems and customers with impossible delivery demands).

The team took these ideas to heart, and in the days that followed, they continued to discuss the differences between strategic and survival mode and to pose questions to Alex. Some members of the team, like Sara, the controller, were already attuned to strategic thinking; others seemed curious but uncertain. In any case, Alex didn't want the team leaders to turn their backs on solving the persistent problems du jour, he wanted them to see the problems from a strategic perspective. He knew that wouldn't be easy: They were an elite team of problem solvers, and they enjoyed the rush and sense of camaraderie they got from banding together to put out yet another fire. As a result, they tended to overlook even shorter-term strategic opportunities because they'd never been challenged to make systemic improvements to the way things were done in Dallas. Whatever the reasons—the neglect of the old management or the deteriorating plant—the team leaders would need to start looking beyond the near horizon.

From the moment he agreed to take responsibility for the Dallas plant, Alex knew that he was in it for the long run. In eight weeks, he became familiar with many of the glaring problems and discovered how resilient the staff were and how much faith they had in Alex's mission. There was no magic formula. Success would require several years of dutiful, disciplined, dedicated effort.

To kick-start the process that was set to launch in two weeks, on Alex's first day back in Dallas, his approach would be simple:

- Employing a few tools and templates, like the Strategy Engine diagram he had shared earlier, to help the team conceive a future-oriented plan and execute on it while coping with the daily problems that are part of ongoing operations.
- Leveraging the team leaders' natural strengths—drive, daring, agility, perseverance, and the ability to see the big picture, among others—to help them acquire the habits of strategic leadership.
- Investing time wisely to focus on the essentials and defer, delegate, or dismiss secondary issues.

It felt good, Alex thought, to have his hands on the levers of the future, one that would benefit everyone connected to the Dallas plant and, potentially, the entire PSI family. All that remained was getting back to Seattle, saying goodbye to friends and colleagues, and moving his family down to Texas. To give himself a chance to mull over his plans without being interrupted by day-to-day distractions, Alex decided to take four days to drive home. That would afford him just enough solo time to review his game plan, take stock of the team leaders who would be spearheading the strategic journey, weigh their talents against their limitations, and consider ways to help them learn from one another—all while traveling through landscapes he loved and enjoying a much-deserved break from the routine. It sounded like a win–win situation. Alex planned to waste no time getting started.

6 | The Art of Ownership

The Story: Robert

On a brilliant morning in the last week in July, Alex backed out of the driveway of his leased condo in Dallas, eased his SUV into traffic, and headed west. For the first time in nearly two months, his destination wasn't the PSI plant in a sprawling industrial park north of the city or the Dallas/Fort Worth Airport for the three-and-a half-hour flight to Seattle for a weekend with Julie and their two sons. Today, he was setting out for Seattle by car, a trip of well over 2,000 miles. He had packed just enough clothing for the next few days, and his favorite mountain bike was mounted on the rear. Ten days from now, he'd be returning with the entire family to Dallas. While the family settled into the house they'd rented near Grapevine Lake and Julie and the boys prepared for the opening of school, Alex would usher in Phase Two of The Plan to transform PSI Dallas.

Fifteen minutes later, he was passing through Irving, where Robert, who was filling in as plant manager in Alex's absence, grew up. The morning shift wasn't due at work for another hour, but Alex was certain Robert was already on the production floor, debriefing the overnight shift leader and reviewing the schedule for today's production runs. He had been head of operations in Dallas for more than four years, so Robert was the logical choice to run the plant for the next week. And yet, Alex suddenly found himself worrying whether the pressure would prove to be more than the young man could handle.

Robert, whose childhood home was a short walk from the old Texas Stadium, the Dallas Cowboys' long-time home field, was a lifelong fan who attended nearly every home game and was glued to the TV when Dallas played out of town. Although he played soc-cer in high school, somewhere along the way he caught the Texas passion for American football. Perhaps that was due to his time playing the trumpet in the school band that entertained the crowd during halftime at every one of the team's games. Alex noticed that

Robert relished playing a supporting role; to him, success often meant opening up possibilities for others that benefited everyone. He thrived on teamwork and never sought the limelight.

Fresh out of high school, Robert went to work on the production floor at the Dallas plant when it was run by the previous owners. Disciplined, steady, and meticulous, within a few years, Robert had worked his way up from apprentice to operator, and from there to lead operator, trainer, and shift leader. When his operations manager retired, Robert was the unanimous choice to succeed him. He was popular with his entire production team. After all, he'd worked side by side with most of them for years and was quick to share his knowledge and tutor new hires and older employees who were mystified by new manufacturing methods, processes, and best practices from around the world.

Despite some recent attrition, the team retained its well-deserved reputation for being staffed by hypercompetent operators. Robert's efforts to bring out the best in every worker were largely responsible for their standing in the plant. He seemed to have a sixth sense about his people, the equipment, and how to fine-tune the schedule to compensate for the Dallas plant's shortcomings due to its outdated technology. He knew when to step in and coach people and when to let them solve problems on their own. Kim in human resources helped out by finding the best training programs, and Sara, the controller, always found room in the budget to invest in helping the plant's top-flight production people keep up with new methods and technology.

Robert loved his work, but he knew that without a college degree, he would probably never advance beyond the plant floor. Early on, he enrolled as a part-time student at a Dallas-area technical college. He often worked the overnight shift in order to take courses that weren't available to evening students, especially advanced chemistry and software applications. Now, he was midway through a Bachelor of Science program in management at UT–Arlington.

Alex noticed Robert's drive and dedication from the start, and he applauded his ambition. He suggested that he apply for partial tuition reimbursement from PSI, which subsidized the cost of courses that enhanced employees' job performance and knowledge of their fields. Encouraged by Alex's interest in his education, Robert started talking about his aspirations with such enthusiasm that at one point, Alex smiled and said, "Sounds like you're after my job."

"Oh, no, sir," Robert replied, but then, seeing Alex's friendly expression, he added, "At least not right away."

The two of them had a good laugh and, ever since then, Robert paid even closer attention to Alex's approach to running the plant and engaging with the staff—especially the team leaders. Sometimes it almost felt to Alex that Robert might be doing field research for a case study in one of his management courses. But he knew the truth: His eager operations manager wanted to improve his already-good relations with the production staff, and he was also curious for clues to what Alex had in mind for PSI's future. He knew that significant changes involving personnel, culture, processes, and systems were about to unfold at the Dallas plant. Robert understood that this was going to be a big deal and was determined to be part of it.

In fact, it was Robert's openness, along with his determination to do the best possible job for the plant and the staff, which told Alex that Robert might be the right person to run things during his absence. Operations was also the largest department—running three shifts a day—and this played into Alex's decision, as did the fact that production had the single greatest effect on Dallas's bottom line of any function in the plant. But these weren't the decisive factors.

Alex had considered appointing two other team leaders to take responsibility for the plant in his absence: Jordan, head of engineering and the plant's technical star, and Sara, the controller, who had the deepest administrative background of the entire leadership team. Jordan was certainly qualified, but Alex didn't want to distract him from the three new projects he and his staff were working on. As for Sara, Alex realized that she would back Robert up if Melissa or Victor at the home office raised questions about budgetary items.

He had other motives as well. What better way to throw a spotlight on Robert's sense of ownership, he thought, than putting him at the helm during a critical time? He saw that the team leaders rallied around Robert to support him in his interim role, but he wasn't sure that spirit would survive once things returned to normal. Despite their heartfelt camaraderie, the silo mentality was still alive and well on the team. Some windows might have opened a bit wider, but no one was showing signs of tearing down the walls.

Halfway to Amarillo, near the ghost town of Medicine Mound, Alex stopped to stretch his legs. When he checked his phone, he found one brief, upbeat message from Robert: "Happy trails, boss! Come back soon," and he knew that all was well at the plant, at least this morning. He got back behind the wheel.

Alex pictured Robert presiding over the production floor—a large space that housed machines designed to convert granules, pellets, and powdered polymer into plastic components and composites used in industry, medical devices, consumer products, and dozens of other applications—and knew that the area would be pristine. The busiest part of the building, the production floor was a showpiece that Robert prided himself on that attracted new customers to the plant and brought existing customers back as reliably as the spreadsheets that demonstrated Dallas's dedication to being a low-cost, high-quality manufacturer and trusted supply-chain partner. Whenever anyone praised him for running such a tight and tidy ship, Robert unfailingly shared credit with Maintenance; but Alex knew that Robert's eagle eye and tireless effort were the real reasons behind Operations' ability to impress. Robert had succeeded in infecting the Operations crew with his zeal for a workplace that fostered productivity, efficiency, quality, and safety.

Alex mused, "Why can't we export these values to the other leaders and their teams as well?" After all, everyone at PSI Dallas, from the front office to the loading dock, has a vested interest in how well our products function, especially those used in sensitive applications like medical imaging, laboratory equipment, and aerospace. Dallas needed a leadership team focused on the long-term health of the entire organization, not just isolated departments. If we cultivated the spirit of ownership in every employee—create an entire plant of owners—Dallas would thrive and flourish. If not, it would risk suffering the fate of Medicine Mound, destroyed by fire and forgotten.

Traffic was light on this weekday morning, and Alex was moving faster than he'd anticipated as he continued northwest towards Amarillo. Suddenly, however, he noticed a low, dark cloud taking shape in the distance and remembered that dust storms were common in the Texas Panhandle. A minute or two later, the sky cleared again, and Alex breathed a sigh of relief. The ominous sight got him wondering whether things were still calm on the production floor in Dallas, where severe disruptions could strike as unexpectedly as storms here on the high plains. At the plant, people tended to use the homespun term train wreck to describe this type of interference. Whatever the word, strategic thinkers always kept one eye peeled on the horizon, just as expert surfers never turned their backs to the ocean. Threats have a way of sneaking up on you.

Alex recalled the train wreck that struck the plant during the week he spent with Robert and his crew on the production floor and lasted, in fits and starts, into the following day. It began when a ladder toppled into a molding machine after a worker, who had climbed up to clear a blockage in a hopper full of plastic pellets, lost his footing. No one was hurt, but production came to a halt until the machine could be readjusted. After it was restarted, someone noticed that the machine's safety guard had been damaged, and more valuable time was lost while a maintenance crew repaired it. Compounding the problem was the fact that Maintenance was short-handed that day; one person was out sick and another was on vacation.

The next morning, the monitoring software failed and production again ceased until nearly noon. Toward the end of the shift, the dust collector malfunctioned and combustible dust was released into the air. When granulated polymer is being pulverized, it creates a fire risk; polymer dust is highly flammable and can ignite and even explode under certain circumstances with little warning. All production had to be halted until the dust could be removed and a new dust collector could be installed. Work did not resume until well into the second shift.

Over the two days, it took six shifts to produce what Dallas normally turned out in three. But by the end of the week, Operations had cut the deficit in half. Alex knew that Robert's deep concern for the plant's success was largely responsible for the fact that Operations succeeded in making up the ground they'd lost. He saw Robert poring over reports and revising schedules in order to make sure customers would be receiving their products as scheduled. Meanwhile, two young operators resigned, saying that they couldn't see a future at the plant, and Alex feared that these departures might demoralize other workers and encourage them to leave, too. But no one followed them. Robert spent more time than ever on the floor with his employees, calming and reassuring them. The log book showed that twice that week, he returned to the plant to spend time with the midnight-to-eight shift, and the shift leader told Alex that even when Robert wasn't on site, they talked on the phone. No matter how early Alex arrived at work during that stretch, it seemed that Robert was already there.

By Friday, it was starting to look like the plant would make its deliveries on time. Still, Robert's vigilance didn't relax one iota. Alex applauded Robert's sense of responsibility, but he didn't want him to burn himself out. Catching Robert as he headed to his office from the production floor, he suggested that now that things were back on track, why didn't he think about knocking off early that afternoon? Robert's reply surprised him. "At the end of a week like this one, I want to keep an eye on things. My first concern is safety—making sure no one gets hurt. Pressure makes some people careless, and we work in a dangerous environment, surrounded by flammable and potentially toxic substances. Beyond that, I have to keep the plant running to meet our production targets. Maybe I'm not a stockholder, but I am a stakeholder."

My goodness, Alex thought. *This guy cares as much about this place as I do. Maybe more. He wants a better future for himself, sure, but also for his team and all the rest of us who work here.*

What Alex said was, "You pulled off a minor miracle this week. You've earned the right to sleep in tomorrow."

As he replayed the conversation in his mind, Alex saw that he was nearing the outskirts of Amarillo. He would stop for lunch and check in with Robert from the restaurant. Today, he wasn't worried about train wrecks.

Ownership Close-Up

In our work helping leaders create and apply strategy at every level of the business, we have found that people are most successful developing and implementing strategy when they think and act like owners. Successful strategic leaders, then, have a keen sense of ownership. This notion of thinking and acting like an owner is crucial; organizations need to be filled with leaders and employees who are fully responsible, act with greater empowerment, and care deeply about and believe in the mission or purpose of the business. Too often, employees and leaders are disengaged and disconnected from the business and their place in it. As a result, they don't fully invest themselves in helping the organization reach its full potential. Organizations that nurture a sense of ownership in their leaders and team members find that the organization's talent becomes its competitive advantage. The best thing about an ownership culture is that it forges synergy and reduces frustration, because people feel compelled to take charge in a healthy way and are genuinely interested in the well-being of the whole organization. When people look out, up, and beyond their immediate responsibilities, things naturally begin to run more smoothly—and who doesn't want that?

In our story, Robert thinks and acts like an owner. He feels connected to PSI and the Dallas plant and understands how his role genuinely supports the whole plant's success. Strategic leaders like Robert not only own responsibility for their piece of the business, they are also highly interested in the long-term success of the broader organization. Let's look more deeply into the minds of this type of leader and explore five guiding principles and the actions that underlie an ownership mentality.

Principle 1: Understand How the Business Works

A leader with a strong sense of ownership doesn't just care about getting the job done. While this is a very important part of what they do, they are also concerned about the success of their team, other teams in the organization, and the business as a whole. Good owners have a genuine concern for the welfare of the entire business. They have a broad, holistic mindset and are acutely focused on aligning the efforts of their team with the other functions in the business. They strive to be knowledgeable about the whole business operation and stay in touch with everything that's going on so they can find ways to actively participate in the company's success. Drawing on their knowledge of how the organization works, they are able to break down silos and work across boundaries. They don't need to be told what's important. They don't wait to be told what to do. They don't need someone else to give them direction. They already have a pulse on it and understand how they can move their team forward—and then they do. Being proactive and making it your business to stay well-informed helps you make the right moves, introduce important changes more effectively, and improve processes that align with shared business goals. Asking yourself a simple question like, "What do I need to know that I don't know already?" can go a long way toward sparking this fruitful line of thinking.

Owners recognize that what they do in their part of the organization, whether big or small, has a real impact on all of its stakeholders—including those who have actually invested their hard-earned capital into the business and are counting on a return. These leaders take the time to learn and internalize the organization's mission, vision, and key priorities, and they really understand how the goals of their department, business unit, or function can play a role in moving the enterprise forward. They are actively interested in learning about many essential aspects of the business, including these:

- How the organization makes money.
- Who the end customer is and what they need now and will need in the future.
- How they will benefit when the company wins.
- How their function links into the organization's value chain of activities.

Feeling a bit lost or unsure about how you can contribute to your organization's strategic agenda is not uncommon. If you find yourself in this situation, do your homework, read the tea leaves, and make a concerted effort to gain a complete picture of your organization's key priorities and where the business is headed. By stepping back and taking a careful look at the bigger picture, it's pretty easy to get a sense of the organization's current and future plans and what truly matters most. Paying attention to the messages that come from senior management or other parts of the business, as well as reading your organization's publications and industry literature, can give you a lot of precious information. Trust us: Your competitors and rivals are trying to track your organization's strategic plans and moves. Why wouldn't you do the same?

Taking advantage of the great sources of information that you have at your fingertips will help you see how you fit, why you matter, and how your unique contribution to the business will affect both the short- and the long-term performance of the whole organization. And armed with that knowledge, you will be able to anticipate what is coming, make better decisions, and create meaningful goals and plans for you and your team.

Because they understand how the business works, leaders who feel a sense of ownership also have the capacity to place the broader interests of the business above their own. We acknowledge that this may require some short-term sacrifices and may even cause some pain. It can be tempting, and can sometimes be easier, to be inwardly focused and seek to maximize one's own self-interest. Occasionally, we might feel inclined to worry only about ourselves, but there will be times when you'll need to overcome that urge. At some point, we guarantee that you and your team will need to do something that is contrary to your own personal interests. Being an owner means learning to be somewhat selfless and having the presence of mind to understand the effects that your choices have not only on you, but also on other team members and the broader organization. In the interest of increasing your personal level of ownership, strive to be a little more perceptive and really take the interests of your organization to heart. In our story, Robert spends extra time at the plant during a particularly difficult week. Even small acts of ownership like these are easy to spot, and the results of the ownership mindset tend to be evident across the entire organization. We think you will be pleased with the results of your efforts in this area.

Principle 2: Unleash the Entrepreneurial Spirit

Think for a moment about business owners. What are they willing to do? Most will do just about anything necessary to produce the results needed to ensure that the business will prosper. This is what we call entrepreneurial spirit. People who embody entrepreneurial spirit have some skin in the game. They know that when you work hard, good things happen more often. They are optimistic about the possibilities that the future holds and are motivated to turn ideas into action. Their relentless commitment drives them to work smarter and go above and beyond the minimal requirements of the job. This is called discretionary performance. When you kindle an entrepreneurial spirit, your heart is fully engaged—not just your mind—and it shows up in both your attitude and in the actions you take. You dive into strategic initiatives and strive to do your best work. You consistently go the extra mile, but especially when you're in uncharted territory. An entrepreneurial spirit is especially important when it comes to sharing a strategic direction or introducing bold changes. To get people's hearts and minds engaged, they have to feel that you—their leader—are genuinely interested in and optimistic about the possibilities that the future holds.

Here are a few tips and suggestions to get you started fanning the flames of your entrepreneurial spirit:

- Rehearse what success looks like in your mind so it guides your day-to-day thoughts and decisions.
- Free yourself from the idea that you are nothing more than a transactional employee filling a role. You are not just one more pair of hands! You have an important contribution to make, and your organization has entrusted you with a piece of the business over which you have stewardship. Act like your neck is on the line. In reality, it probably is: If you are unable to add value and make a relevant contribution, you put yourself and the organization at greater risk.
- Find the unique strengths or special capabilities that you bring to the table and leverage them any way you can. This will allow you to contribute in ways far beyond what you need to do just to keep your job. Engaging your strengths gives you a feeling of belonging and a sense of place—and those unique qualifications help you make a real and lasting difference.

By and large, our success comes not so much from what we do (our jobs), but from how well we attempt to do it (our passion for our jobs). As we execute on important priorities and consider tomorrow's possibilities, our passion for and ownership of our work plays a significant role to help us achieve the future we desire.

Characteristic 3: Be Fiercely Accountable for Results

We love this quote from Pat Summitt, the former University of Tennessee women's basketball coach: "Responsibility equals accountability equals ownership. A sense of ownership is the most powerful weapon a team or organization can have. You get leadership when you take ownership." This articulates another important characteristic of strategic leaders: They are accountable for results. Most leaders have a clear line of sight to the results they need to achieve in the short term. The key difference is that a strategic leader's focus goes beyond the short term and extends to include long-term milestones and outcomes that will get them where they want to be (or avert potential problems down the road).

At its core, accountability is taking responsibility for achieving results, regardless of the obstacles or barriers that may be standing in the way. When it comes to being proactive and executing on long-term goals, you can bet that you'll make some missteps and encounter resistance along the way. That's just how it goes. What really matters is that when you make mistakes or miscalculations, you make no excuses, take responsibility for the error, and figure out a workaround. In this context, a workaround is the next-best solution or a different approach. For example, you might scale back your plan, take smaller steps forward, or try an unconventional approach. Quite simply, you own up to your contribution to the problem and then figure out a new way forward; you knock down the barriers that are preventing you from achieving your desired results.

When you establish a culture of accountability through your own behaviors and actions, you will foster heightened levels of autonomy, trust, and personal accountability within your team, which will engage your team members in entirely new ways.

Principle 4: Take Ownership of the White Space

Every organization has white space—sometimes a little and sometimes a lot. The white space is a visual description of the activities, tasks, roles, or responsibilities that are not clearly defined by the organization's current roles and responsibilities, boundaries, or structure. The white space is where important tasks, critical activities, or problems that often fall between the cracks reside. They aren't assigned to or managed by anyone in particular, and because they don't specifically belong to anyone, they often get ignored and go undone. With these descriptions in mind, you can probably come up with an example of a white-space issue that is causing some kind of dysfunction in your organization almost immediately. While it can be frustrating to a lot of people, strategic leaders can sometimes do their best ownership work in the white space. When these leaders see a problem or opportunity that could impact the future and it falls squarely in the white-space arena, they take initiative and step forward to do something about it. They see possibilities for long-term improvement that exist in this space and are willing to work outside of their silo and bridge the gaps between functions or teams in order to make a difference. If only people would claim greater ownership for the white space, imagine how much less often we would hear, "That's not my job," or "I'm not paid to do that." Imagine the competitive advantage you could create.

The white space is ripe with strategic and innovative opportunities that can be game changers for organizations over the long run. It transforms organizations and teams into well-oiled machines and drives out frustration and inefficiency. Be willing to extend yourself beyond your natural or formal boundaries. Look for roles that need to be filled, jobs that need to be done, and processes that need to be developed to create greater synergy in the business and help move it forward.

Principle 5: Be Fiscally Responsible

The final, important trait of leaders who think and act like owners sometimes gets overlooked: It's their earnest respect for the organization's financial well-being. Just like the actual owners of the business, these leaders are prudent with and mindful of the organization's resources. Prudence was described as one of the four cardinal virtues by Plato, and although the word prudence is usually defined as being cautious, frugal, or using discretion, the roots of this word are fascinating, and telling: Prudence comes from the Latin word *prudentia*, which means foresight. As we've mentioned, having keen foresight is a central part of your leadership responsibilities. You and your team members are stewards of the organization's resources; you must make decisions and solve problems with this responsibility in mind.

We have found that one way to fine-tune this ability is to treat the company's funds and resources as though they were coming out of your pocket. When defining what it means to be an owner, the CEO of one of our clients provides a simple, yet compelling, example. He challenges the members of his organization to take on a greater sense of ownership by saying, "If you are buying an air-line ticket, booking a hotel, or reserving a rental car for a business trip, think about the cost as though you are buying it personally." Thinking of the company's resources in this way will help you look at them in a new light. Some people view strategy as simply find-ing new and creative ways to spend less and sell more. Regardless of your personal take on it, we would argue that everyone in the organization needs to be aware of the financial condition of the organization. When people understand how the company makes money, it becomes easier for them to understand how everyone can affect the team's and organization's growth—in either a positive or a negative way.

The Benefits of Ownership

Thinking and acting like an owner makes work more meaningful, rewarding, and enjoyable, but it also provides people with the grounding needed to sustain a strategic journey—both when times are good, and when they're tough. So, hold up the mirror for yourself and your team. Do you see a group of business owners looking back at you?

7 | The Art of Tenacity

The Story: Mya

Early on the first afternoon of his trip, Alex stopped at a restaurant just off the interstate, ordered a sandwich and a salad, and scrolled through the morning's email messages and his favorite news sites while he ate. Over coffee, he decided it was a good time to check in with the plant and dialed Robert's number. At first, Alex detected a hint of nervous excitement in his operations manager's voice. When he asked about the two large orders that were scheduled to ship by mid-week, Robert informed him that production was on schedule for both. In fact, he said, everything was running smoothly, and his tone grew more assured. Alex smiled, thinking, *I've put the right guy in charge.*

A few minutes later, Alex was back on the highway, heading west across a landscape that stretched endlessly before him. It was so flat, in fact, that he imagined he could see the Sandia Mountains of New Mexico in the far distance. He felt as if he were moving across a blank artist's canvas. *That's why I wanted to take the time to drive back to Seattle*, Alex thought. Driving gave him a chance to step back from the day-to-day distractions of the plant, get a fresh perspective, and plot a course that would transform Dallas and ensure that it played a key role in PSI's future. Especially when stepping into the middle of a troubled situation, it was too easy to get trapped in firefighting mode. That wasn't going to happen to him. From the first day he arrived in Dallas, Alex found himself counseling his team, "Sometimes you have to slow down to speed up." That's exactly what I'm doing this week, he thought, and laughed because right then, he was driving at 75 miles an hour.

When he revealed to the team in Dallas that he would be gone for 10 days and they might occasionally have trouble reaching him when he was passing through some of the lower 48's more-remote areas, half of them tried to talk him out of the road trip. They urged Alex to fly home, pack up his household and family, and fly right back to Dallas. He was surprised at how quickly they'd come to depend on his presence, especially since he'd bent over backwards during these first eight first weeks to avoid interfering with their current management styles or decisions. It was obvious, however, that they'd begun to rely on his leadership nonetheless. He wasn't swayed by their efforts to persuade him to change his mind about the drive. To the contrary, he hoped his absence would give them an opportunity to look at their own roles with fresh eyes.

The one team leader who vocally supported Alex's decision was Mya, the manager of quality. Mya didn't often go out of her way to express agreement with others, but she respected people who made firm decisions and stuck to them. Alex, she saw, had thought through the pros and cons of the trip and was committed to entrusting the management of the plant to his six team leaders for this limited period of time. She wasn't sure what his aim was—to test their ability to work out whatever problems arose, to support Robert in his interim role as manager, or something else—but she was confident that her department could hold its own and she relished the authority Alex had invited them to embrace.

A fast-talking, energetic New York native, Mya's colleagues sometimes teased her about being a Yankee. In fact, her story is much more complicated. Her parents emigrated from Rio de Janeiro, and Mya and her two daughters visit her grandparents there every summer. Besides being fluent in Portuguese and English, she also speaks excellent Spanish. About one quarter of the Dallas staff is Latino, and Mya's ability to communicate with them in Spanish as well as English gave her great credibility with production workers and others who have a significant effect on the quality of PSI Dallas's products.

Mya is in her mid-thirties. Six years ago, her husband was killed in an explosion at a plant where he worked as a chemical engineer. Hazardous chemicals, improperly stored, had ignited, the warning system had failed to activate, and dozens of workers had been trapped with no chance of escape. Since then, Mya has been a single mom to her two daughters, ages 11 and 7.

Alex was sure that Mya's relentless pursuit of quality and her conviction that safety and quality are linked owed a great deal to the tragic circumstances of her husband's death. He has often heard her say that "Quality is safety built into the product and safety is quality built into the process." Until Dallas recruited her four years ago, Mya was a quality assurance specialist at a plant that manufactured precision aerospace parts, an industry where a malfunctioning component can have disastrous consequences. Since she joined the Dallas staff, she had established a focus on quality as a way of life throughout the plant. Only when she detected that her colleagues were backing off from quality principles or being distracted by flavor of the month programs did she display impatience with the other members of the team. Alex heard her say that defects were like self-inflicted wounds; Dallas could lose out to its competitors merely by delivering enough substandard products to lose the confidence of its customers.

Alex compared Mya's tenacity and persistence in embedding long-term quality initiatives at Dallas to the determination shown by a marathoner, and so did many of Dallas's customers, including her former employer. Companies purchasing Dallas's products felt that Mya represented their interests at the plant as well as those of her own firm. In aerospace applications, polymer's advantages over metal, including its lighter weight, adaptability to unusual shapes, and freedom from corrosion, have made it a highly desirable material. Mya's presence in Dallas helped attract its first orders from her former employer, and since then, other aerospace suppliers have become customers as well.

It didn't take Alex long to see the value of Mya's ability to sustain quality processes and systems. He did admit, however, that she sometimes got carried away by her enthusiasm, and others sometimes misread her dedication as inflexibility. A few weeks earlier, production completed its first run of a custom dynamic component for an important customer. The quality technician announced that the parts were too far out of spec and would have to be scrapped. Operations disagreed, and Engineering backed them up, insisting that the devices were within acceptable tolerances and could be shipped as scheduled.

In an attempt to resolve the dispute, Mya introduced a unique perspective. She compared the component to a surgical instrument or an implantable device like an artificial hip joint. "Imagine that a surgeon is operating on one of your close friends or relatives," she said. "How would you feel if a part we manufactured failed because we had allowed it to slip through our quality inspection? How would the manufacturer—our customer—react? Would they trust us with their future business? Would anyone?"

Her point struck a nerve with many. Everyone agreed that Dallas could achieve better quality for this customer. Even when Jordan, head of engineering, displayed diagrams showing that technically, the components might be passable, the entire team agreed that shipping questionable products didn't reflect Dallas's quality standards and sent the wrong message about what the plant was capable of—and what it stood for.

Needless to say, Mya was pleased with the decision to pull the parts back. The cost of scrapping an entire run was substantial, but Alex had no doubt that it was the right thing to do. He praised Mya for her patience and resolve in maintaining the quality standards they were all dedicated to providing. He summed up the outcome by observing, "Working together, we can prevent mistakes. When we operate in isolation, things are likely to fall through the cracks. Better safe than sorry."

Alex knew that Mya could appear uncompromising. That was a coachable issue; it would be relatively easy to help her bring some balance to these dilemmas and avoid letting her ego get wrapped up in the decisions that were made. On balance, however, he was grateful that she had found the courage to say what needed to be said. She stepped up on other occasions as well, such as when she came to the aid of Walter, the supply-chain manager, when a supplier tried to persuade him to accept a shipment of raw materials that were of questionable quality. Mya was a smart player, and Alex knew she had the capacity to develop a bit more diplomacy to soften her zeal in championing Dallas's quest for quality at every stage in the process.

The tempest over the quality issue was still running through Alex's mind when, just after he crossed the New Mexico state line, he noticed the check engine light glowing on his dashboard. He chuckled when he found himself thinking, *What would Mya do?* Alex knew that the warning light was often triggered by nothing very serious, but should he risk breaking down in this desolate area? Mya, he remembered, liked to describe strategy as a decision filter. To make the best, most-strategic decision, you needed data. In this case, that meant finding out why the light was on.

Alex's GPS located an auto-repair shop in Tucumcari, 20 miles to the west. There, the mechanic plugged a diagnostic tool into the SUV's onboard computer. The issue was low brake fluid, an easy-enough problem to correct, but one that might have meant trouble, especially on the steep, mountainous downgrades that lay ahead on his route. When he got to Seattle, he would have the dealer check the car's hydraulics, but this afternoon, he silently thanked Mya as he drove back toward the interstate highway. Back in Dallas, he knew, she was the plant's walking, talking check engine light, the person who could be counted on to catch potential disasters before they left the plant. Could she also begin to appreciate other perspectives and work with PSI's other teams to find ways to integrate quality at every stage of its processes? That approach could potentially reduce defects to close to zero. It would be the next challenge.

For the remainder of the day, Alex's progress was undisturbed. He decided to spend the night in Santa Fe, left the interstate southeast of the capital, and drove north through the foothills of the Sangre de Cristo Mountains. When he reached the city, he could see the sun setting behind the Jemez Mountain Range near Los Alamos. He checked into La Posada de Santa Fe, a three-minute walk from the historic plaza. The sprawling hotel incorporates a nineteenth-century mansion built by the merchant Abraham Staab that popular legend claims is haunted by the ghost of his wife, Julia. Julia loved the house so well, the story goes, that she couldn't bear to abandon it. Mya was a little like Julia, Alex mused: She will never abandon or compromise her goal of creating a culture of quality in Dallas. This old hotel may be the perfect place, he thought, to exorcise any ghosts opposed to Dallas's transformation that were still lurking within the walls of the plant.

Tenacity Close-Up

All good leaders and managers need a healthy dose of dedication and determination to excel in their roles and responsibilities. But from our analysis of great strategic leaders, mere dedication doesn't quite do it justice. There is something special operating inside of these leaders that goes beyond determination and commitment. We believe that the differentiator and hallmark of a true strategic leader is tenacity.

Tenacity is a strong word, and it takes strength to have the endurance and focused intensity necessary to execute a strategy and act proactively. During our workshops on this topic, we like to say that strategy is a plan to win. In this context, tenacity is the intense will and total commitment needed to achieve results over the long run. Strategic leaders understand what winning means for their function and for the organization. That's a given. The key is not only knowing what winning means but also remaining consistent and steadfast as the action plan rolls out. We don't see it as blind tenacity but rather informed tenacity, or the resolve to make things better for the organization in specific ways and in spite of obstacles, inconveniences, or the effort that will be required.

As strategy evolves and gains traction, it is a leader's endless determination and conviction that leads to breakthroughs and real progress. Strategic leaders have an intrinsic motivation to win burning like a fire inside them, and they find satisfaction in the journey they take to reach their goals. They are unwilling to settle for the usual outcomes, and they consistently push beyond basic expectations. They have an unstoppable will to do whatever it takes to move forward, build momentum, and create a following of supporters.

The interesting thing about executing on long-term priorities is that it requires a delicate blend of both tenacity and agility. Strategic leaders need to be adaptable in order to exploit emerging opportunities and flexibly respond to challenges, but they also must be exceptionally tenacious and focused to sustain critical changes and see things through. In a lot of ways, strategy is more like a compass than a turn-by-turn road map. A compass points you in the direction you want to go. Then, each day you have to harness the courage and will needed to calculate the right moves and find the best way around the potholes or unexpected obstacles that can stop you in your tracks. To be sure, detailed plans are immensely helpful. But the human qualities of tenacity and agility will help you navigate through the twists and turns (and the uncertainties and surprises) that are difficult to predict but a part of every journey.

There are two main components of tenacity: drive and perseverance. Let's take a closer look at these two elements and learn how you can develop higher levels of personal tenacity.

Drive

Tenacious leaders are tireless. They have the capacity to work hard, but they also have the stamina necessary to keep existing activities and tactics going while simultaneously supporting experiments on new ideas and implementing game-changing initiatives. One manager we work with said, "It's like fixing my bike while I'm riding it." That is exactly what it takes to be a strategic leader. You have to be able to make the needed progress on today's demands while fixing things and preparing for the future. Focusing on short- or long-term wins alone is not what will allow forward-looking leaders to achieve the results they want. You need discipline and the patience to delay immediate gratification in order to achieve future desired outcomes. This can obviously be a little tricky. You have to be mentally committed to the strategic-change process and have the raw passion and conviction to succeed, both now and in the future. You have to start the process, stay on top of it, and apply a strong work ethic as you figure out the practical actions you'll need to take to make a strategic difference. At times, pressing through and overcoming the inevitable disruptions, resistance, and obstacles takes tremendous effort.

Without the fortitude to set your ideas into motion and the drive to finish what you start, you can end up frustrating people on your team. It's easy to wear people out. Let's face it: Just keeping up with the day-to-day routine and all the problems associated with it can be exhausting. But when daily demands are compounded with the need to invest some energy, time, and resources into a strategic transformation as well, at times, it can feel a little grueling. What people need to see is your personal commitment to the strategic journey. No one wants to set out on an ambitious expedition without knowing that their leader has the steely resolve and determination needed to finish it.

On a few occasions, we have witnessed tenacity taken to an extreme. Some leaders have trouble letting go of bad ideas, and it can become a battle of wills against other, competing ideas. When this happens, people become so attached to a particular direction or path that they are perceived, even by their supporters and allies, as obstinate and unreasonable. This out-of-control tenacity is counterproductive because it creates an environment of defensiveness and fear and does nothing to push the strategy forward. Don't let your plans and ideas for the future be strangled by ego or pride.

If you do, you risk losing the critical mass required to achieve the momentum necessary to finish the voyage. A better approach is to demonstrate your confidence and create a belief among members of your team or organization that the strategic priorities are right, achievable, and essential to the business's future prosperity. You can't expect your colleagues and team members to be committed, focused, and tenacious themselves unless you model that behavior yourself and lead the way. Strategic leaders create a culture where people are encouraged to be part of something exciting; part of a cause bigger than themselves. When people see that you are driven, tenacious, and have an inspired purpose, they become more confident in your leadership. They know you won't give up, even if the method or the route to your destination changes, or if a better opportunity or target comes into focus.

Some leaders develop a drive to succeed early in life. It seems to come naturally to them. Maybe it was born out of an artistic talent or an extraordinary athletic ability; perhaps it came from working on a farm and doing manual labor to pay the bills. Other leaders, faced with a challenge or special opportunity (like Mya in our story), may develop this drive later. What's important to remember is that any leader can learn to be more tenacious. Developing greater tenacity begins with asking yourself what really motivates you deep inside. Then, when you embark on a new agenda, remind yourself, on a daily basis, why this endeavor is important to you. When you start to overthink things or come up with reasons why you shouldn't proceed, you have to stop yourself. Take some time out. Write your story down and prepare an elevator speech about what you are setting out to do so you have something concise and thoughtful to share with others. Another way to develop higher levels of personal tenacity is to find role models who have pushed through in spite of overwhelming odds. Thomas Edison said, "Many of life's follies occurred when people didn't realize how close to success they were when they gave up." Study what tenacious people do and analyze how you might be able to incorporate some of their practices into your own life. And at the end of the day, simply knowing what your priorities are and giving them the attention they deserve will help you achieve your desired results.

Perseverance

No matter how much you try to avoid them, obstacles and adversity can and will enter every aspect of your life at some point. Dealing with problems—both large and small—is part of everyday life. The same is true when you are shaping the future. The reaction we have to an obstacle is strongly influenced by our thoughts and beliefs about the obstacle itself or other hurdles we have to overcome. If a person's thoughts and beliefs about the challenge are negative or dysfunctional, their behaviors are likely to be self-defeating—even destructive. They behave like victims of the circumstances and fall into a vicious cycle of complaining, assigning blame, and dodging responsibility. However, when a person's thoughts and beliefs are more flexible, optimistic, and realistic, their behaviors and emotional reactions are more likely to produce positive outcomes. We can't choose the types of adversity we will encounter, but we can choose how to react.

When you embark on something new or bold, some forces are likely to manifest that will deter you and oppose your plans. A tenacious leader has the capacity to stay the course, regardless of the interference they encounter, the adjustments they will inevitably need to make, or how difficult the end goal may be to achieve. They have the strength of will to press forward and overcome disruptions, resistance, and obstacles of all types. In a way, the challenges they face actually seem to strengthen their resolve to achieve what they desire, and they forge ahead even when circumstances are less than ideal. Art Turock, a renowned business author, says, "There is a difference between interest and commitment; when you are interested in doing something, you do it when circumstances permit. When you are committed to something, you accept no excuses, only progress . . . you act in spite of resistance."

Strategic leaders believe in the notion that quitting is not an option. When it comes to being proactive and making strategic choices, you need to expect a bumpy ride and move through the turbulence in spite of it all. You have to be pain tolerant and able to rebound from criticism and vocal naysayers, scarce resources, fatigue, or whatever else is standing in your way. Developing this quality requires that you learn to pace yourself and fight one battle at a time.

A sustained strategic effort usually requires prolonged mental effort and tangible action; look at it as a marathon rather than a sprint. Ultimately, you have to find the pace that will allow you to endure. As in Aesop's famed fable *The Tortoise and the Hare*, steady wins the race. When the going gets tough, strategic leaders rely on their stamina and continue to move toward their goal at a steady pace. They aren't deterred by hardship and they don't give up. They are quietly confident that they can overcome obstacles and setbacks by tapping into the larger purpose that inspires them to act. They know that initial failure is just a dress rehearsal; it allows them to shake out all the kinks so that they can be successful when it really matters.

The Tenacity Formula

As we have studied strategic leaders in our training and consulting practice, we've identified five specific tips and suggestions about leading with tenacity that we would like to share with you. As you review these insights, think about how they apply to your particular situation and how you might incorporate these concepts into your own style of leadership:

1. You are more likely to be tenacious and driven when you have defined the right objectives or goals. As you strive to be

more proactive in your work, spend your precious time and energy establishing a clear picture of the outcome you want. Then, focus on producing some early wins with the desired outcome in mind. Don't get obsessed with or waste time and resources on things that aren't within your sphere of control. Remind yourself why you believe in what you are doing and have a singularity of purpose as you work on each action step in your plan.

2. Approach your long-term responsibilities and goals with optimism and a can-do attitude. We recognize how much easier it is to focus on tactical activities; there is urgency associated with them, and crossing items off the immediate to-do list brings a sensation of accomplishment. Remind yourself that with many strategic initiatives, the payoff may be gradual. In addition, there will always be people who can't see the possibilities or just don't want to move outside of their comfort zones. Anticipate some resistance from others. It is normal and natural for people to be somewhat fearful of change, but do what you can to help them grasp the larger purpose of the change and buy into the strategic plan. Stay committed as you move through the resistance. This might be compared to encountering a steep grade ahead sign on a road trip. Shift gears and be prepared to take the hill more slowly than you might have liked. As your plans and objectives begin to unfold, people will get on board. They may even end up providing the added push you need to reach the summit. This is a time to call on your strength, determination, courage, and convictions. It becomes the gas in your tank and gives you the energy you will need to reach a tipping point.

3. Picture how you feel when you've spent a lot of time mapping out a journey, and once you get on the road, you see a detour sign. After getting over the initial disappointment, most people recognize that they will have to take the detour or find a new route to their destination. When you encounter adversity or setbacks related to your strategy—and you will—immediately step back, assess the situation, brainstorm some different approaches you could try, make an informed decision, and move forward. The key is focusing quickly and efficiently on what you need to address and taking what you've learned and

applying it to your next steps. Reversing direction or treading water until conditions are more in your favor are okay choices, too. You have to learn to take detours in stride. There will be uphill battles early on, so maintain your composure, adjust your timeline if necessary, and find ways to steamroll over the obstacles. Keep in mind that there might be times when you have to improvise, so trust your instincts, draw on your experience, and find a way through the drama and challenges that can accompany strategic change of any kind.

4. If you want to make something happen, you'll need to enroll the support of people who are both busy and accountable because they are the ones who will help goals and strategies come to fruition. One manager we work with often says, "I am always busy, my plate is full, I encounter special challenges all the time, but I thrive on change." We're sure that your plate is full, too. When taking on something new, you can counteract feeling overwhelmed by setting up milestones and breaking the game plan down into incremental steps that others can support you on. Focus on the critical-few elements that offer the highest return on your investment. Any time you see a road work ahead sign on a road trip, it can feel a little deflating, right? On a strategic journey, you can counterbalance this feeling by celebrating progress and small successes along the way. This will help you sustain momentum over the long haul. Some leaders we have studied wait for the final outcome, only celebrating when their teams cross the finish line. These leaders tend to be less successful with their strategic projects because their teams lack the fire or passion needed to win. Team members in these situations are inclined to complain and resist more in the beginning, and they contribute to long-term plans and goals only when they are formally compelled to do so. Your strategic contribution will have much more meaning for you and your team if everyone can find some joy in the journey.

5. Some strategic initiatives designed to get you to a better place may be smaller and more modest, requiring only minimal effort and attention. Others may be big and audacious, requiring significant effort over a much longer period of time. In either case, you have to pace yourself and recharge your batteries

along the way. Your tempo really matters; when acting with urgency and drive, you have to strike the right balance. If you try to do too much too fast, it may take a toll on you and your team and lead to costly setbacks. On the other hand, if you do too little or move too slowly, you may miss opportunities to make a real difference. One leader we work with leaves her office a few hours early once a month, typically on a Friday. She uses that time to visit a museum, attend a concert, or do something else to refresh her mind and renew her energy. Another manager told us that his favorite leadership tool is the three D's:

- Delete
- Delegate
- Defer

This concept is important, especially for tenacious leaders. The philosophy behind the three D's is this: Some things need to be deleted or eliminated to create space for strategic activities; some things need to be delegated in order to get others involved in the strategy and free you up for the things that are a priority for you; some things simply need to be delayed. The whole point is that you have to make some smart choices about where and when to expend your energy. You can't be all things to all people. At times, it can be tempting to chase every shiny object that comes along, and it's easy to bite off more than you can chew. Work to prioritize the opportunities you see and pursue them in an intelligent way. We are not suggesting that you work more hours or take on more stress. It's not about working harder; it's about working smarter and getting ahead of problems and potential issues down the road.

Mastering Tenacity

Right now, in this moment, you are capable of achieving much more than you may think. Let your passion for long-term success drown out the doubts in your mind. Let it provide the momentum you need to push through. The opportunities are there. Find your zone, fire up your tenacity, and go for it! When you do, you will see the true rewards of thinking big—and acting even bigger.

8 | The Art of Risk

The Story: Jordan

The next morning, Alex rose with the sun, checked out of his Santa Fe hotel, and ate a quick breakfast at a café just off the plaza. Always a light sleeper, this morning he wanted to get on the road as early as possible. If he took the most direct route, he would cross over into Colorado by late morning, pick up the interstate south of Provo, Utah, and make it well into Idaho before nightfall. In that case, he'd be home in Seattle the day after tomorrow. He was eager to rejoin Julie and the boys and help with the final preparations for their move to Dallas.

At the same time, he felt he had unfinished business with respect to the past eight weeks in Dallas. The solitude of the road was the perfect terrain for working through it. Besides, he was about to leave the flat, mostly arid terrain he'd been driving through for the high country of the Central Rockies and was looking forward to seeing some scenery that was new to him. Weighing his options, Alex saw in his mind's eye the poster hanging on the wall behind the desk of Jordan, the plant's engineering manager: "Life isn't about avoiding risks—it's about taking calculated ones," it read. That slogan summed up Jordan's approach in a nutshell, Alex thought. He was never skittish about experimenting or trying something new, whether it was an unproven manufacturing process or an untested but promising material.

This morning Jordan's adventurous spirit challenged Alex to make a risky choice of his own. He had time for one bit of daring. Should it be hiking or mountain biking the Colorado Trail near Durango or kayaking on the Colorado River? At that moment he recalled an essay by the nature writer Edward Abbey, who described Canyonlands National Park as "the most weird, wonderful, magical place on earth—there is nothing else like it anywhere." Alex had often thought of wandering through this wilderness of mesas, arches, canyons, and pinnacles sculpted over eons by the Colorado River. Today he would see it with his own eyes.

Pondering his adventurous choices reminded Alex of Jordan's situation, and now that he had seen Jordan operate with his own eyes, it was clear to Alex what made Jordan special. Jordan had managed Dallas's engineering group for at least 10 years before the PSI acquisition, and Alex thought of him as the focal point of nearly everything having to do with the plant's output. He was nicknamed Magic Jordan because of his uncanny genius for turning the most complex customer demands into products that could actually be manufactured. Jordan graduated from Caltech with honors but left before completing a PhD; while conducting his dissertation research, he decided that he preferred making things to the more abstract pursuits of academia. His studies in chemistry and manufacturing engineering comprised an ideal foundation for his professional specialties: new applications for polymers, composite materials, and automation of manufacturing processes. After more than two decades in industry, he continued to participate in technical conferences and to publish papers on advances in automation technologies, polymer-product fabrication, and the development of new materials.

Early on, Alex perceived Jordan's vital importance to the Dallas plant's ecosystem, but his first impression was of someone a bit arrogant and standoffish, a savvy industry veteran who wouldn't be quick to welcome the new manager who'd parachuted in from the West Coast. Within a few days, however, he realized that he had misread the signs: What initially struck Alex as arrogance was simply Jordan's confidence in his abilities, and his seeming reticence was in fact a fierce focus on bringing innovation to Dallas. That passion had been stifled by the previous management when it decided to cut costs and milk the plant for cash before selling it off. Alex had initially suspected that Jordan might have nursed hopes of becoming plant manager himself, but nothing could have been further from the truth. In fact, during one of their early conversations, Jordan revealed that during the previous two years, while the old management neglected the plant, he had reluctantly filled the leadership vacuum and didn't enjoy it. "Not only didn't I acquire a thirst for power or control," Jordan said, "the experience reminded me how much I prefer the risks one encounters working on something new—a challenging prototype or novel process—to running a business. I'm grateful those dark days are finally over with."

To his eight-person engineering staff, Jordan seemed more like a brilliant mentor than a manager. One of the younger team members even told Alex that working with Jordan was like participating in a graduate seminar, "only from one week to the next you're not sure what the topic's going to be." As the weeks of Phase One of his onboarding plan passed, Alex noticed that other departments relied on Jordan's encyclopedic knowledge of the technical aspects of their industry as well. Robert, the head of operations, frequently consulted Jordan about production problems, especially when the products involved unfamiliar materials that responded to heat and pressure differently from more-traditional polymers.

When Alex saw how unreservedly the entire staff trusted Jordan, he understood how essential this quality was to shaping and executing a long-term strategy in Dallas. Trust among team members and across departmental borders was a crucial prerequisite to planning the future, the psychological bankroll players must have in order to compete in the leadership game. Day after day, Jordan earned his colleagues' trust by applying his analytical abilities and technical knowledge to solving their problems as if they were Engineering's most-pressing concerns. Often, he encouraged them to risk taking new approaches, measured and well thought out, where the potential payback was high.

He didn't always succeed in convincing them. But risk-taking would be a critical element of Dallas's long-term strategy calculated to make the plant indispensable to PSI. Jordan's example would be invaluable across the organization, but especially in Engineering. That department would have to make even bolder moves than it had been accustomed to doing, especially if they were to attract new business and win more contracts for custom, high-margin products.

Some of the reasons for such extreme caution in the past may have been the attitude of the previous management, who focused on cost savings above all else. But Alex also knew from past experience that many engineers were risk averse: If they couldn't eliminate most of the risk, they tried hard to minimize its likelihood and potential impact.

Early in his career, Alex had shared that caution-first outlook and sometimes advocated for it. Then, several years before he joined PSI, he briefly joined a California venture-capital firm as a technical analyst. These were aggressive investors, fearlessly searching for promising startups. An original, but unproven idea and a forward-looking management team were often all it took to persuade them to open their checkbooks, and they betrayed no fear of failing. In fact, their mantra was "Fail fast and fail often, but fail cheap."

The best venture capitalists were also excellent assessors of risk, and they knew better than to try to eliminate it completely. Exposure to that environment changed the way Alex looked at risk, and how he decided when a risky venture was worth pursuing. To assure Dallas's future as part of PSI, he would have to raise his own risk-assessment and risk-taking mastery another notch or two. It felt good to have Jordan along as a partner—and possibly a mentor—in this search for the right balance.

When new tools, methods, or designs are adapted for production, however, the equation changes, and risk takes a back seat to rigor. Then the engineer's role is a delicate balancing act, and Jordan excelled in this arena as well. A technical link between sales and the customer, on the one hand, and plant production and quality, on the other, the plant engineers ensure that the design conforms to the specs and the limitations of the materials and can be produced on the facility's machinery. Last but not least, it must be profitable. A high-level concept that looked good on paper, or even in early prototype, sometimes turned out to be too difficult or too expensive to manufacture. The plant engineers' challenge was to find a way around such obstacles, in pursuit of the 3 *P*s: performance, producibility, and profit.

Prior to the acquisition, Dallas served its own customers exclusively and handled both the conceptual and production-engineering work in-house. As a result, a nearly seamless transition was possible between the two stages of new product design, one that often anticipated potential problems and eased the handoff to Operations. How well would Jordan and his engineering staff adapt to the PSI system, Alex wondered, where initial designs were executed at headquarters and then sent to the plant engineers for refinement and implementation?

Jordan was used to running his own show, and Alex had already seen home-grown designs developed by his Dallas team that rivaled what the engineers at PSI's New Jersey headquarters did. A year ago, Jordan pulled off a major coup for one of its largest and most-demanding customers, an aerospace-parts manufacturer: For a component whose shape changed in response to temperature fluctuations, he employed a shape memory polymer (SMP), replacing the metallic shape memory alloy (SMA) the customer had previously used. Because SMPs are more elastic, lighter, and cost less, the customer got a lighter-weight, more-reliable product at a lower cost—a double-barreled benefit in the highly competitive, cost- and emissions-conscious aerospace industry.

Thoughts about Jordan's unique qualities continued to run through Alex's mind as he turned off onto the state road leading to the Needles District of Canyonlands. He decided to pass up the challenging hundred-mile-long White Rim Road mountain-bike trail in favor of exploring one of the park's dozens of canyons on foot. On a hot July day, the more arduous route might have proven a risk too great.

This afternoon, Alex knew he would encounter few other hikers along the trails. At the visitor's center, he picked up a trail map and drove to the Elephant Hill trailhead a short distance away. With an ample supply of drinking water and some trail mix in his knapsack, he set off on foot for Druid Arch. Compared to the Grand Canyon, Canyonlands might seem a bit tame, but the landscape reveals its own splendors. Carved out of layered sandstone by the Colorado River, the landscape is crisscrossed by trails that lead hikers past red-rock spires, desert-hued cliffs reflecting the bright sunlight, and occasional salt domes, as well as through deep canyons covered in sand and loose rocks. Averaging just eight inches of rain per year, wildflowers in this area bloom only in the spring and early fall. In summer, vegetation is limited to brush and scrubby piñons and junipers, but the colors in the iron-rich Cedar Mesa Sandstone formation surprised Alex. Such variety, Alex thought, even with the limited palette of this landscape. At that moment, Alex was struck by the similarities between the desert scenery before him and his team: A similarly diverse set of natural abilities would allow them to turn the Dallas plant into an amazing organization together.

At the upper end of Elephant Canyon stands the Druid Arch. To reach it, Alex scaled the steep ladder bolted to the rock face and scrabbled across the rocky final stretch of trail. Soaring 450 feet above its pedestal, the spectacular, isolated natural formation got its name from its resemblance to the monumental megaliths at Stonehenge. In its way, the Druid Arch was as awe-inspiring and almost as regular in its proportions. But it was the Colorado that did this, Alex had to remind himself, not human effort. It just happened, flowing water shaping the sandstone over eons; a marvelous accident. Alex knew the change he would inspire from his team and in the plant would take more thoughtful effort; it would take some time to mold and shape the team so it could reach its full potential.

As he retraced his route to the trailhead, Alex marveled at the natural wonders he'd just seen and the ancient engineering wonder from which the Druid Arch took its name. The engineers of Stonehenge were cunning risk-takers as well, he reflected, hauling massive 25-ton stones a distance of 20 miles, maneuvering them into perfect orientation with the sun during the summer and winter solstices, and securing them in positions they've held for more than four millennia. In Dallas, he thought, we can succeed on a more modest scale. He knew there would be some detours, adventures, and maybe even some dead ends as the Dallas team explored the future. Regardless, Alex felt certain that Jordan's knowledge and the example he set as a smart risk-taker would help secure a place for Dallas in the PSI network of businesses.

When Alex turned for a last look along Elephant Canyon, the sun was halfway between its meridian and the horizon. Although he could no longer see the Druid Arch, he imagined the sun's rays passing through its main opening, as at a Stonehenge solstice ritual. Smiling, he walked back to his car and headed toward Moab. The afternoon's adventure had been well worth the detour, but now he looked forward to a refreshing shower and relaxing in his hotel room.

Risk Close-Up

As we have said, there is a short list of essential qualities that make a leader fundamentally strategic. One of those core characteristics is a leader's perspective on taking risks. After working on the topic of strategic thinking for many years, we have come to the conclusion that strategic leaders' risk tendencies can set them apart from other leaders when it comes to making a unique contribution to the business. This stems from the fact that in order to make visions, goals, and strategies come to life, you need to be courageous and willing to take a risk with things that are new, bold, or different. We have found that in order to be proactive and support the organization's efforts to grow and transform, neither leaders nor individual contributors can continue to do the same things in the same ways. As the world changes, you will need to find new, different—and sometimes wholly unfamiliar—solutions to problems, both old and new. This will ensure that you'll have a lasting impact on the business. But to venture into that territory, you have to take some calculated risks—and that definitely means you'll need some courage.

Whether we like it or not, we live in an uncertain world that is fraught with risk. We're swimming in it, and much of the time, we aren't even aware of the risks all around us. The funny thing is that even people who try desperately to avoid risk by hunkering down and putting their heads in the sand are inadvertently taking a risk; standing still comes with its own kinds of dangers. We could still be struck by lightning while taking cover under a tree. We could still fall ill, even if we see the doctor regularly or feel perfectly healthy. In actuality, we take all kinds of risks on a daily basis, whether we think we are making that choice or not. Even if we wanted to, it would be impossible to eliminate risk from our lives entirely. What we can do is choose to supplement the ambient risk that's all around us with some smart, calculated risks that can be expected to provide favorable outcomes. In short, we have a choice about how we choose to work with risk and the way we view it.

Risk: Good or Bad?

There are plenty of leaders out there who are overly obsessed with maintaining safety and security. They are so committed to ensuring stability and so terrified of taking even a small risk that they lose out on great possibilities. Other leaders may take the bait and chase after really bad ideas because they look good at face value but end up having short odds and poor potential return on investment. Some leaders all too frequently view risk in a negative light, for a variety of reasons. This really isn't surprising given the way risk is defined in the Oxford English dictionary:

1. A situation involving exposure to danger.
2. The possibility that something unpleasant or unwelcome will happen.

3. A person or thing regarded as likely to turn out well or badly.
4. A person or thing regarded as a threat to something in need of protection.
5. A thing regarded as likely to result in a specific danger.
6. A possibility of harm or damage against which something is insured; possibility of financial loss.

No wonder risk is seen in such a pessimistic light! When we look at risk through this lens, the reasons why some leaders want to avoid risks at all costs become very clear. The Internet and television news are filled with stories about the hazards of contemporary life. We have seen some estimates and studies indicating that more than 40 percent of news articles focus on the negative risks to which we are exposed. Small wonder, then, that some leaders surrender to their fears and allow themselves to be paralyzed by the loss and pain that could accompany a risky initiative. In contrast, forward-thinking leaders operate with the mindset shared by Franklin D. Roosevelt: "The only thing we have to fear is fear itself." These leaders get in the driver's seat and take control of their situation—and they do so courageously, knowing that they will need to take some risks along the way to create a better situation for themselves and their teams.

Profile of a Smart Risk Leader

Really good strategic leaders operate with the belief that they can't afford *not* to take risks. The people doing their same jobs in rival organizations certainly are. The key differentiator is that these leaders think deeply about the risks they could take and go after the right risks in a smart way. They have to do their jobs better than the competition; this is how effective risk leadership can be a source of competitive advantage. Being a risk leader means looking for ways to play offense rather than defaulting to just a defensive game plan. These leaders look for ways to leverage, pursue, and capitalize on high-value, game-changing opportunities, even when there is some risk involved. They look at bad risks and seek to minimize, mitigate, or avoid them. They also have the capacity to look at high-potential risks and embrace, seek, and pursue them. The key is discerning the type of risk you have in front of you.

You need to be brave to accept the fact that even a good risk could go off the rails. Strategic leaders tend to have a higher pain threshold than most. It allows them to make smart bets and accept the outcome, even when it isn't the one they desired. These leaders play the probabilities, knowing they will win some and lose some; that's just the way business works. Getting greedy and expecting to win every time is just foolish—and it will result in many rude awakenings. Strategic leaders, like Jordan, understand that it's important to be realistic, and that there is a correlation between the level of risk and the level of return: When there is no risk, there can be no return. In order to realize any kind of return, you have to first be willing to take a risk.

How Risk Works (or Doesn't Work) in Organizations

Unfortunately, far too many managers and leaders in today's organizations wonder whether they're really supposed to be taking risks. They fear that if they take risks that don't end well, they'll suffer negative consequences. An organization's cultural beliefs and assumptions can lock leaders' thinking in the status quo. Some of the beliefs that people hold about risk can create a formidable wall. This wall of assumptions can block our ability to make important changes and exploit risks that could lead to new and powerful opportunities, as shown in Figure 8.1.

Do these sound familiar? Brick by brick, these thoughts and notions build up into what can eventually become an impermeable wall in our minds. This wall prevents us (and our teams) from being open to trying new things and new approaches. In order to see

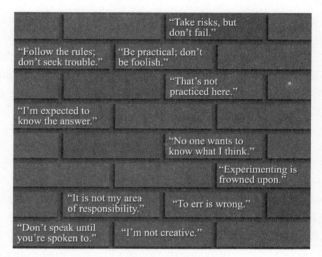

Figure 8.1   Wall of Assumptions

what's on the horizon, gain a better vantage point for seeing the possibilities, and bravely try out something new, we have to break down these walls. Let's look at six common sources that make the bricks of this wall in most organizations.

1. Risk Beliefs and Values

Every person is different, and we all have our own personalities. Our assumptions, beliefs, attitudes, and mindsets strongly influence our outlooks on and preferences related to risk. There are three main risk styles:

1. Risk seeking
2. Risk neutral
3. Risk averse

When looking at this list, what is your gut reaction? What is your natural stance when it comes to risk? How might that be influencing your results in a positive or negative way? Have you lost out on an opportunity in the past because you were unwilling to try something new or unknown, or are you the type to seek out those opportunities? It's okay to experiment, coach yourself, and challenge your assumptions. Taking even small steps will help you develop greater flexibility when it comes to risk.

2. Patterns and History of Success with Risk

Behavior that has been rewarded in the past is likely to be repeated in the future. As such, people who have reached some level of success by being risk averse are prone to remain risk averse, while those who have been successful risk seekers are likely to continue to seek risks. If you tend to be more risk averse by nature and have been successful with this approach in the past, you will need to work a little harder to experiment with risk. Take little steps. By starting small, you'll be able to see that you can also be successful by taking calculated risks—and that risk-taking often leads to even more significant positive outcomes than you'd get from avoiding risk altogether.

3. Frame of Reference

When thinking about things like goals, plans, decisions, or strategies, we perceive risks differently based on whether we see those things as having a positive or negative impact on us, our lives, our careers, and so on. It is always a little easier to take a risk on something that you feel will really benefit you if you are successful—and it will be a little harder when facing a possible outcome that you perceive as less desirable. Ask trustworthy people what they think, calculate the odds, and aggressively pursue opportunities that have attractive benefits.

4. Group Influence

Although we may not be conscious of it, our risk behavior often conforms to the prevailing patterns of the group or situation we are in, and individuals commonly assume riskier positions while in a group environment. This is called groupthink. Groups who fall into this trap may not challenge one another's assumptions—either when venturing outside of the traditional ways of operating or assessing the value of staying well within their boundaries.

5. Familiarity and Experience

Situations that feel familiar to us (or that we have more experience with) help us to more accurately assess the risk involved, and we will act accordingly. However, because our world has become increasingly unpredictable in many ways, we will always have to deal with some uncertainty. In order to help tip the scales in our favor, strategic leaders must anticipate and prevent unexpected and unwelcome surprises. As we've said, working through the uncertainties we face in unfamiliar territory takes a lot of courage, but we know that it can be done—and that you can do it.

6. Organization Control Systems and Culture

An organization's processes, controls, and especially its culture heavily influence whether you and others feel comfortable taking calculated risks—or not. If the culture of your organization isn't supportive of doing things in new ways or thinking outside the box, you may find yourself being overly cautious. On the other hand, if the culture of your organization is open to experimenting with new ideas and taking smart risks, you may feel more encouraged to seek risk out.

These factors have tremendous power over our propensity to pursue strategic initiatives that might involve some inherent risk. But with some self- and situational awareness, we can be more conscious of the variables that affect the choices we make—something that's especially important when we're making decisions that will affect the future we create for ourselves and our teams.

Stepping Up

Your strategic ideas and plans will go nowhere unless you step outside of your comfort zone and take the risk needed to start something new, bold, or different. Keep in mind that when it comes to creating a strategy for your Business-within-the-Business that supports the organization's overarching strategy, you probably aren't dealing with a situation that's tremendously risky. Under these circumstances, your relative level of vulnerability is actually pretty low. However, if you still find yourself being less risk tolerant than you should be (or simply want to fine-tune your perspective on risk), we can offer a few tips. Strategic leaders, like Jordan, consistently engage in behaviors like those that follow to manage their mindset and potential risks more effectively.

1. Any time you are faced with a situation, opportunity, or issue, recognize that there may be potential risks and uncertainties involved, and then define the degree of severity of each one. This provides you with a more honest, less-emotional sense of the true risks that are present. By taking this analytical approach, you often find that the level of risk involved may be lower than you initially thought.
2. Weigh the benefits along with the costs. We know this sounds rudimentary, but many leaders fail to do it. The benefits are the payoffs or rewards that will be the result of accepting the risk; the costs are what you could lose if the risk doesn't pan out as you'd hoped. Knowing how you will profit from

the risk or what it could cost you will always lead to better decision-making and analysis. And even if taking the risk doesn't end in the way you'd hoped, you'll still reap the benefits of learning something—which is an integral part of the process.

3. Strategic leaders have an explorer mentality, and when it comes to risk, they carefully scrutinize their information as they forecast scenarios and design experiments. This means that you have to be educated about the effect that taking the risk will have on things like the time, costs, and resources involved. This is different from the benefits and costs we examined earlier. With benefits and costs, you are examining the likely results (the final outcomes). Here, we are looking at how things might unfold as you take action on the risk. This precious data will give you everything you need to construct a realistic mental picture of the likely positive scenarios that could develop, as well as the scenarios that are more negative. Armed with this information, you have two options: You can choose to pursue or accept the risk, or you can choose to avoid, transfer, or prevent the risk from happening altogether. As you weigh which course of action to take, remember that in some situations, you don't have to put everything on the line. Taking the risk incrementally, one step at a time, is sometimes the best way to go.

4. The final thing we would like you to consider is exercising your courage muscle when you can (and it makes sense to do so). Dr. Leonard Zunin, a researcher and author in the mental health field said, "Courage is seeing your fear in a realistic perspective, defining it, considering alternatives, and choosing to function in spite of risks." Making some subtle adjustments to your mindset about even the simplest risks will put you in a stronger position; when you find yourself facing risks of more significance later on, you can use your new perspective. We like to think of it as a "Why not?" frame of mind. It sounds something like this:

   - Why not try something new?
   - Why not use a different approach?
   - Why not reach out to the customer?
   - Why not look at this in a different way?
   - Why not think ahead and get prepared?

Learning to look at risk as an opportunity on your path to new, better, and great—as opposed to a path to potential failure—will help you shift your mindset in a more productive direction. Being dedicated to your vision, values, and goals, while being honest about reality, provides you with the guardrails needed to stay on track as you try new things.

A Note About Failure

We like this thought from former Supreme Court Justice William O. Douglas: "Adventure calls on all faculties of mind and spirit. It develops self-reliance and independence. Life then teems with excitement. But man is not ready for adventure unless he is rid of fear. For fear confines him and limits his scope. He stays tethered by strings of doubt and indecision and has only a small, narrow world to explore."

Real strategy requires some level of risk, and as with any risk-taking endeavor, there is the possibility of failure. There is no doubt that failure will be uncomfortable. But it also creates constructive tension, which is often the catalyst for significant progress and breakthrough ideas. Reframing your outlook on failure in this way can help you see that setbacks, missteps, or even accidents really aren't failures at all. Unless you are willing to accept the potential for failure and the benefits of constructive tension, it will be difficult to get ahead of the curve and move into a more-strategic mindset. As you increase your tolerance for risk, you will start to notice that leaders who have this quality are able to restrain their desire to create a plan that is perfect and utterly free of risk. Instead, they are willing to venture out into less-familiar territory and, if necessary, allow things to get a little messy at points along the way.

The fear of failure or taking risks is one of the biggest impediments to making real progress. If you are in constant fear of making a mistake, you *are* making a mistake. Quite frankly, if you want to be successful and you strive to lead your teams in a more strategic way, taking risks is just part of the equation. As you look toward the future and create long-term plans and goals, work hard to overcome the paralysis that can be caused by fear of failure. We know it can be hard, but if you pull it off, you will be better equipped to serve the people who have a stake in the success of your business, and they will look to you to lead them into the future.

When it comes to taking calculated risks in an effort to shape the future for yourself, your team, and the organization, you need to tap into your inner drive and personal tenacity to face down those fears and challenge yourself to drive the change that will pave the way to the future you desire. The good news is that developing your ability to be courageous when faced with risks and unknowns becomes easier with regular practice. Strategic leaders recognize that they need to be a force that intentionally produces results rather than simply reacts to situations that arise. But to become that force, they have to be willing to step out, take a risk, stare the possibility of failure squarely in the face, and bravely stand their ground.

9 | The Art of Agility

The Story: Kim

After hiking the length of Elephant Canyon under a blazing sun and dining on beef tenderloin at a local diner in Moab, Alex planned to turn in early. He was impatient to get home to his family, but he reminded himself that these few solitary days on the road were allowing him to gain invaluable perspective on his Dallas team's ability to shape the future. From his hotel room, he sent Julie photos of the spectacular vistas he captured along the trail, and then talked with her by phone to report on his progress and promise that he'd be in Seattle in a couple days.

Early the next morning, Alex was the first guest in the hotel's sunlit breakfast room. Always a morning person, he peacefully replayed the previous day's adventure in his mind and looked ahead to a long day behind the wheel that would take him through southern Idaho into Oregon. If this were an ordinary workday in Dallas, he would be reviewing yesterday's unresolved issues and setting the agenda for the 10:00 A.M. staff meeting with his team leaders. Two hours from now, he knew, Robert would be opening the daily plant leaders' meeting; unless there was a crisis, Alex wouldn't hear anything about what they discussed until late in the afternoon, when he called to touch base with his team.

Soon enough, Alex knew, he would be back in the chaos that was business as usual at the plant: to-do lists that always seemed to add new items faster than he could check the old ones off; conference calls with Melissa, Victor, and other senior managers; meetings with suppliers and customers; visits from safety regulators; unending people issues; and following up on corporate audit items. Until Alex moved into middle management in Seattle, he rarely gave much thought to how important having a network of relationships was to the success of an organization, and how many of his colleagues and employees would cross his path every day now that he was plant manager. In Dallas, where the sense of turmoil and transition was unusually close to the surface, he sometimes felt almost like a character in a Shakespeare play: Some days, people's personal tragedies and thwarted ambitions competed for center stage; other days, they miraculously managed to keep things afloat, despite everything seeming to go wrong at once. Once or twice he half-joked to Kim, the HR team leader, that they should write a good-humored parody entitled *PSI: Love You*, to be performed at the plant's annual holiday party.

Of all the team leaders in Dallas, Kim was the one who greeted every triumph with enthusiasm and every setback with perfect composure. The week after Alex took over in Dallas, several experienced operators resigned in the space of a few days, leaving production short-handed. At the time, Kim was busy collecting data for the strategic-staffing projection for Alex. But the moment the immediate crisis broke, she joined forces with Robert to sustain production-run rates for all three shifts by juggling work assignments. The result was that Dallas made every one of its delivery dates that week. To bring the staff back up to full strength, Kim dipped into her database of applicants and her network of area recruiters and, almost overnight, Robert was able to sign up several experienced new people. Then, she dove back into her original project for Alex and handed it to him on schedule, as if she'd had nothing else to do that week. When Alex praised her for helping to turn things around so quickly without losing sight of the bigger, long-term picture, Kim brightened. "If we can dig ourselves into a problem," she replied, with just a hint of pride in her voice, "we can dig ourselves out."

That was Kim's M.O. She tackled the unexpected problems that came out of nowhere, without allowing even a code red crisis (and in Dallas there were plenty of those) to obscure her view of her long-term strategic priorities. What's more, she toggled between tasks with the ease of a photographer switching between wide-angle and telephoto lenses. It was as if Kim's mental camera was outfitted with an infinitely flexible zoom that responded automatically to the demands of the moment.

After that incident, Alex knew that he had an invaluable ally in Kim—and just as importantly, he recognized that her adaptability and agility were talents the entire leadership team needed to acquire. When he asked Kim where her maneuverability and drive came from, she credited her father, who had emigrated from South Korea in the 1970s. By that time, his native country was well along in its industrial development, but Kim's father believed that greater opportunity and mobility existed in the United States. Hardworking and ambitious, he soon met and married a young American woman and started a successful wholesale food business. Kim was the eldest of three children. By the time they took their first steps, she and her siblings had already been encouraged to be flexible and self-reliant. All three were driven to make the most of their educations. In college, Kim majored in psychology and then attended law school. After a short stint at a law firm, she switched to HR and found it the perfect way to combine her two interests.

Thoroughly informed about local workplace issues and regulations that were constantly in flux, Kim helped Alex get up to speed about the legal and safety standards for manufacturing in Texas. Her value to the Dallas plant went far beyond her mastery of rules. She was largely responsible for the policies that turned Dallas into a worker-friendly environment. To name just one of her innovations, Kim developed a creative benefits package that managed to keep costs within bounds. Now that Dallas was part of PSI, she was integrating the local and corporate benefits so as not to jeopardize the perks the plant's employees currently enjoyed.

Most valuable of all were Kim's contributions to Dallas's training and development programs: keeping people current with state-of-the-art technologies and organizing teams from Engineering and Operations to facilitate knowledge exchange and improve communication among those who design manufacturing processes, tools, and products and those who have to bring it all together on the shop floor. Initiatives like these were morale boosters, and they also helped engineers and operators anticipate problems with new orders before they go into production.

Alex noticed that Kim was not only bold when it came to responding to a new idea, venturing into unfamiliar territory, or trying something creative on her own; she also instigated collaborative efforts between people from different departments—as when she persuaded Maintenance, Engineering, and Operations personnel to team up to improve communication and reduce waste. Whatever problems threatened the plant's smooth functioning, Kim's natural tendency was to quickly invite all the stakeholders to share their ideas and come up with a collective response that satisfied everyone. Although she didn't always succeed in securing unanimous buy-in, Alex gave a lot of credit to Kim for having the ability to let go of ineffective practices and procedures and help others work through their fear of change.

Kim's example was essential to Alex's long-term plan for transforming Dallas. No strategic journey follows its initial blueprint from A to Z (or even to B or C); leaders need the agility to respond to obstacles and adapt, just as sailors continually tack into the wind in order to stay on course. Leaders who aren't nimble enough may fail, because once a strategic journey begins, formal plans that are overly rigid tend to go out the window.

Like the best leaders, Kim expected the unexpected. Surprises didn't surprise her, and they certainly didn't deter her from quickly springing into action. She actually seemed to enjoy the challenge of an apparently impossible challenge and was never discouraged. When a direct approach failed, she looked for a way around the obstacle and responded rapidly. Her dealings with people were similar: She might have a heated disagreement with a colleague one day, but the next day, it was just water under the bridge. Every colleague was a potential ally, and every conflict was an opportunity.

Late that morning, Alex left Utah's brilliant red-rock landscape behind and climbed into the Wasatch Mountains. Before crossing into Idaho, he decided to stretch his legs and stop for lunch in

Park City. He promised Julie that he would check out Park City during his drive home; they both liked to ski and thought Park City might be a nice spot for a winter getaway. A few hours ahead lay the wide band of national forests that made up Idaho's green heartlands, and he was starting to feel the pull of the forests, rivers, and coastal waters he had come to love during his years in Seattle. For a moment, he heard a voice whispering, *Do you really want to give all this up for North Texas?* At the same instant, he thought of Kim, always ready for new circumstances and challenges, curious to encounter the surprises the future held. No, Dallas was too rich an opportunity to pass up, a chance to catapult from being a good manager to a true leader, to learn from the leadership qualities of his new team while he also shaped them into a force to be reckoned with within PSI. He didn't want Dallas to be his final stop at PSI, but he did want it to be his next stop.

Agility Close-Up

Agility means many things to people and is used in a variety of contexts in business, sports, and various art forms. Some might reason that leading in an adaptive or agile way is indicative of a leader without a clear direction or leadership style. We contend that being agile is one of the special qualities of strategic leaders and key to accomplishing any long-term objective. Our analysis suggests that agility is a strategic leader's edge when it comes to putting their team in a position to win. In a strategic-leadership context, agility is the capacity to respond rapidly when an opportunity opens up and having the flexibility needed to efficiently make course corrections and execute action steps in a flexible way. Agile leaders are nimble and have a keen sense of how their long-term plans are unfolding so they can move fast when problems emerge or action is needed to jump on a creative idea. They don't defer issues or procrastinate when decisions need to be made. We are not implying that they're impulsive—just that they waste no time making smart, well-thought-out moves. They like to strike while the iron is hot. When you observe these leaders in action, you'll find that they process decisions quickly and avoid being distracted by other things that could dilute their focus on the ultimate prize.

The ability to be flexible and adaptable is often an underrated and overlooked talent. However, it is a necessary part of being proactive. As we've mentioned before, the math is pretty straightforward—if the rate of change inside of the organization doesn't exceed the rate of change in the external business environment, you will lose. Too often, leaders have not fully developed the level of agility and speed needed to address this challenge. We'll call it the agility gap.

You may have noticed that in the leadership-competency models we included in Chapter 1, there is a strong agility theme:

"Anticipates future business trends accurately and responds quickly and effectively."

"Makes decisions to drive long-term success."

"Is insightful and sees things from a new angle."

Some organizations are very clear about this competency and call it strategic agility. These organizations realize that agility is central to driving the business forward. Our findings agree with Brian McGowan, who asserted in a *Forbes* magazine (June, 2012) article "Agility: The Ingredient That Will Define Next Generation Leadership" that "only 10 percent of today's employees have the appropriate level of leadership agility." We have to figure out how to close that 90 percent gap.

You might be wondering how agility is different from some of the other qualities we explore in this book, such as change driver or tenacity. It's a fair question. What we have found is that all of these qualities mutually reinforce one another and are interconnected to some degree. And yet, each quality has its own distinctive attributes. They are subtle but important differences. For example, when discussing the quality of being a change driver, the focus is on effectively spotting important changes occurring in the organization and driving productive change in your area of responsibility so you can remain on the cutting edge. Tenacity, on the other hand, is all about effectively managing your energy and stamina so you can work through challenges and see things through to completion. In contrast, agility is more about the speed at which you recognize and respond to a needed shift in direction. People who compete in yacht races call it "seeing the shift." This might refer to seeing the wind shift, seeing the water's current change, or spotting a competitor's moves. It is all about being quick and nimble as you begin to be more proactive and execute on important strategic programs and priorities.

One of the reasons why we think agility can be a bit challenging to define is because it isn't a single, obvious trait or specific mindset. In our work, we have seen that agility is comprised of five interrelated gifts or talents that work in combination to form this strategic-leadership trait. The following sections explain each element of agility in more detail.

1. Being Built for Speed

Zara is a fascinating global fashion retailer that is recognized not only for its specialty designs, but for its unique and highly successful business model: As you've probably already guessed, Zara operates with remarkable flexibility and speed.

Zara is known as the pioneer of fast fashion. Within as few as two or three weeks after a trend shows up on the fashion runways, Zara will have it produced and in their stores. Their products are shipped to their retail suppliers already tagged—and in some cases, already on hangers—so they can go straight to the store racks, leaving little need for inventory. The retail stores carrying Zara's products typically run very efficiently, and even store managers get in on the action by reporting trends and customer feedback on a daily basis. This information is quickly dispersed to Zara's in-house designers, who sort through it for hot concepts. These new designs are then developed at breakneck speed. With new designs cycling into the stores on a constant basis, customers have a fresh buying experience nearly every time they set foot in a Zara store. Zara has completely challenged the fashion industry's age-old notion of biannual fashion cycles.

Zara is, without a doubt, built on speed. It's the foundation of their culture, but it is also built into their methods, processes, systems, and infrastructure. As a strategic leader, you and your team need to operate a system built for speed, like Zara. When it is balanced with the right level of analysis, speed is the ultimate strategic weapon. Being quick and nimble almost allows you to move forward without a plan—although we aren't necessarily advocating for making that choice. What you do need is the ability to move fast when action is needed and just get cracking. You need to be able to quickly discern the need for an adjustment and rapidly pursue a smart idea; don't let issues fester, or fail to make decisions about opportunities that need to be addressed. Your methods, processes, systems and even the infrastructure of your team need to be positioned to shift quickly when needed. Now, we aren't saying that you should recklessly accelerate through the direction you have mapped out or every part of your plan of action. You just have to know when to take your foot off the analytical brakes and start driving. We think this quote from Joseph Addison, an English writer, sums it up well: "He who hesitates is lost. Swift and resolute action leads to success; self-doubt is a prelude to disaster."

2. Exercising Dexterity

The Latin root of dexterity is closely linked to the very essence of strategy: It means prosper. In our minds, having dexterity allows us to perform with ease and proficiency, which gives us the ability to prosper. Strategically oriented leaders often have a high level of mastery in their chosen profession or field. This enables them to move quickly, but also with grace and ease. They use their intellectual talents to mobilize resources and actions while exploiting opportunities and obstacles that require a rapid response. In our learning events, we call this a person's strategic reflex. This is a clever way of thinking about how you recognize and respond to opportunities, forces, and events that seem to have come out of nowhere.

Leaders with dexterity quickly assess situations and reframe their options, responses, and next moves. They are able to spot the silver linings in otherwise-gloomy situations. They also know when to speed up their efforts so they can outmaneuver the opposition. Skillfully building alliances and seeing the potential of combining forces allows them to take advantage of favorable circumstances. When their luck changes or patterns shift, they recognize it. What may appear random to others, strategic leaders recognize as valuable insights, and they interpret the new developments in their changing world without a lot of fanfare or drama. To the casual observer, these leaders may look calm, composed, and in perfect control—but in actuality, they are working furiously to process the data stream of clever thoughts that are flowing through their minds and make adjustments on the fly.

A few years back, we had the opportunity to work with a fascinating manager, Rusty, who exemplifies dexterity. Rusty is the manager of a pretty sizeable research and development group consisting of 75 highly trained individuals who work in a state-of-the-art facility. Before moving into the private sector, Rusty led a research team at a university. The first clue that we were working with a strategic leader was the thoughtful, well-documented, creative strategy that he had developed for his part of the business. Everyone called it the game plan. The other thing that we found intriguing about Rusty was the fact that all of his internal customers held him in very high esteem. When we inquired about Rusty's relationships with his customers, his fellow managers explained that he was able to effortlessly shift his resources to help the sales team win new business opportunities that had long-term implications. Rusty's group also had another unique strength: They're able to ramp up new programs while still keeping their eye on existing initiatives. Rusty has built partnerships with external labs and academic colleagues; he draws on this network in an effortless, seamless way when a shift occurs and his R&D group needs outside assistance. In all likelihood, there are probably some people in the business who don't know that independent external allies are doing some of the work. This approach allows Rusty's team to attack new opportunities with efficiency and dexterity, and without building internal infrastructure prematurely. Quite honestly, Rusty's leadership is a work of art. He orchestrates all this activity and set up his team's infrastructure, processes, and systems in a way that allows them to ramp up—or ramp back down—in a heartbeat. Strategic dexterity is the perfect way to describe Rusty's ability to pull things together like a master puppeteer.

A lot of managers we have encountered show operational or day-to-day dexterity as they balance competing demands, but far fewer demonstrate the ability to execute on strategic opportunities as well as deliver results today. While not all of us can be as proficient in this area as Rusty, we can all learn lessons in agility from people who can make strategic moves without making a fuss or crippling other programs and campaigns in the queue.

3. Letting Go of the Old and Learning the New

One large, global corporation we observed faces an ongoing and interesting dilemma with its leadership: They have a very well-articulated growth strategy and have become increasingly progressive with their talent-development initiatives because of it. The senior-leadership team knows that they have to operate at the top of their game and establish a more forward-thinking culture in order to head off the competition and reach the level of growth they desire. As such, they have introduced a few new, critical priorities that will position the organization for continued, long-term success and make them an employer of choice in the locations in which they operate. However, we have discovered that leaders in this organization are slow to respond or take quick action on the important changes that need to be made. This situation is particularly challenging because leaders at all levels of the business are at the center of these important strategies and efforts to make the organization better. We were asked to be their partner and conduct an in-depth study so they could better understand why their leaders aren't embracing these initiatives and developing their own supporting strategies in each area of the business. What we learned is that the problem comes down to a lack of leadership agility. These leaders are open to the new ideas being proposed. They recognize that rapid adjustment is essential for long-term success. They've been given all kinds of tools, resources, and support from the home office. Many have even put together supporting strategies and plans on paper. Despite all this, far too many of these leaders lack the agility, speed, and sense of urgency needed to shift from doing things the way they have always been done to doing some new things well. Sometimes this phenomenon is called approach avoidance: On the one hand, change makes sense; but on the other hand, letting go of the familiar, tried-and-true practices that got the organization to where it is today requires agility. And some leaders simply don't have it. Lacking the necessary agility, leaders will fail to seize the day and execute on plans and priorities with speed and nimbleness, and the new, big, bold efforts just drag on and on—and never gain any real traction.

Success with your strategy will require you and your team to assimilate new attitudes, behaviors, and ways of thinking. You have to be agile enough to lead the change and get people to buy in to the new direction or cause. As you play to your strengths and minimize your weaknesses, you will gain momentum and get some early wins that will send a signal to everyone in the organization that big changes are achievable over time, little by little.

4. Shifting between Strategic and Operational Work

Proactive leaders are a different breed because they can fluidly toggle back and forth between completing the daily operational work and developing new avenues to success. Their ability to maintain operational excellence while they shift and devote resources and energy to rolling out the new strategic direction is very sharp. Being able to facilitate this shift is important; in order to achieve strategic goals, you have to allocate some time and energy to thinking in new ways, making decisions, solving problems, and creating new processes. Building a strategic culture can be a dilemma for leaders because there is intense pressure to deliver results now. But when leaders are nimble enough on their own to be operationally effective while simultaneously pursuing the strategic side of their work, they add significant value to the organization. Having the presence of mind to transition back and forth between competing short- and long-term demands is an enormous asset to any organization that wants to remain competitive.

Angela is one of the best examples of leadership agility we have encountered. She is the manager of a finance and accounting team within a business unit of a large pharmaceutical distribution company. She is not a member of the elite senior team; she heads a team that performs the normal activities of budgeting, accounts payable, accounts receivable, and the other accounting-related services that every company needs. When looking in from the outside, it's hard to see anything special about Angela and her team. But when people get to know them a little better, they find that Angela has an uncanny ability to move effortlessly from the everyday, arguably mundane, routine of crunching numbers and cranking out financial data to transforming her team and positioning the organization for long-term results. Not long ago, Angela and her colleagues found themselves embroiled in a fierce battle with their rivals in the marketplace. Her internal customers wanted new and different services. Angela had the presence of mind to realize that in order for the business to compete with their rivals, she would need to continue delivering the services that she and her team had traditionally provided to the organization while the people on her team also learned how to do new things that would make the organization better. She recognized that most of the company's department managers could not easily interpret financial data and make good decisions based on the numbers that Angela and her team provided. Angela's internal customers were good operators and extraordinary administrators. However, Angela saw a strategic opportunity to serve the business in a slightly different way: The organization needed advisory and consulting services almost as badly as it needed traditional accounting services, balance sheets, cash-flow statements, and closed books. She discovered that many managers lacked the financial acumen they needed to know when to pursue an acquisition, where to build a new distribution center, how much inventory to carry, and when to double down and invest in new technology. Angela and her team used this understanding to develop a strategic plan to help leaders use accounting rules, depreciation schedules, inventory-reporting protocols, and other reports to make better decisions and grow the business. Angela knew that her team could make a significant contribution by helping the business improve its financial performance. The true beauty of Angela's work was her ability to switch gears. One day, Angela and her team would be sharing insights and providing advice to internal customers, and the next day, they would roll up their sleeves and close the books for the quarter. She confessed to us that the team found their strategic advisory work to be quite exciting and rewarding (and very visible), but they were also disciplined and flexible enough to quietly perform their traditional functions behind the scenes.

We believe every leader can learn from Angela's example. Shifting your mindset and focusing back and forth between operational and strategic work may not be as instinctive or come as naturally to you as it did for her, but with a little deliberate thought and effort, everyone can find some space in the course of a day, week, or month to make the shift and deliver strategic results.

5. Responding to the Unexpected

Just about everybody knows that when it comes to strategy, you have to expect the unexpected. Even with a crystal-clear vision and the best-laid plans, you will face uncertainty. As such, leaders can't be so committed to a particular direction or plan that they leave no room for flexibility and adjustment. Making some assumptions is just part of finding a strategic target or developing a plan. You can't know everything in the beginning (or ever, really), so you have to keep your eye on the clear and compelling picture of the future you want to create—and then move with fluidity toward it on a daily basis. Whether you have to make wide or sharp turns, adjusting your course along the way allows you to achieve lasting change and capitalize on new developments very quickly. You really have to feel your way through rather than plan your way into a space that nobody has entered before.

Strategic leaders are committed to the current strategy or approach to doing business, but only as long as it works. If the current approach or plan hits a snag or stops working for any reason, they are quick to reevaluate their methods, make decisions, and test responses to the changes they make. These leaders also anticipate a variety of scenarios and devise appropriate contingency plans ahead of time so they aren't caught off guard, should any of those situations unfold. Don't be so committed and attached to your initial plans that you don't leave room for flexibility and changes.

Your Flex-Agility

Most generals would tell you that in the fog of war, people are left to their own devices and even the best-laid plans require some improvisation and flexibility. The ongoing spread of technology and the interconnected (and constantly changing) nature of globalized business require leaders, employees, and the organization to be able to quickly adapt and respond to new needs in the midst of the fog. More importantly, what organizations need is for their leaders, at all levels, to be out on the leading edge by improvising and having *flex-agility*. Agile leaders have an established practice of paying attention to what is working—and what isn't. They keep their awareness engine running by monitoring a continual stream of data. This helps them anticipate and reduce the chances of unexpected surprises, act with speed, and be flexible in their approach. Draw on your experience and learn from the events that are shaping your world, whether those events are small or large, less impactful or paradigm-shaking, or take place in the external environment or inside the boundaries of your team. Remember, you always have to be ready to respond when signals indicate something needs to be examined or dealt with. True, being quick and nimble might feel a bit chaotic, turbulent, or even uncomfortable at times. It's easy to get caught up in the plan you've committed to and become so inflexible that you can't make adjustments along the road. But for leaders who are willing to be more nimble, making adjustments can be very exciting, providing possibilities that only agile leaders can capture and exploit.

10

The Art of Awareness

The Story: Lu

One opportunity Alex pledged to take advantage of as soon as he decided to drive back to Seattle was seeing the Columbia River Gorge, the 80-mile-long gorge separating Oregon and Washington that runs through the Cascade Mountains. Throughout his years in Seattle, Alex and his family had spent many weekends and vacations in the area, hiking, biking, and taking in its natural wonders. To reach the trails near Hood River that he planned to see again, he would have to drive well past nightfall. But the prospect of seeing the morning sun reflected in the river's surface was all the urging Alex needed. He was mentally prepared for a long stretch behind the wheel. It would be worth the effort. At this moment, it occurred to Alex that there could also be long stretches of road between exciting breakthroughs in Dallas. But with the right people on the bus, Alex knew that his team's chances of success would be much higher.

The people at the plant, including the team leaders, came to Dallas from nearly every point on the compass, but only one of them was a native of the Pacific Northwest: Lu, head of the maintenance department, had been born and raised in Vancouver, British Columbia. Like Seattle, Vancouver enjoyed a relatively mild climate year round, and during the summer months, it rained, on average, every other day. To get away from the endlessly overcast, rainy winter months in Vancouver, Lu started vacationing in the American southwest and on the Gulf Coast. On a fishing trip to Galveston Bay, he struck up a friendship with a man who told him about the booming labor market for skilled workers in Texas. As soon as he returned to Vancouver, he applied to immigrate to the United States, was awarded a green card and, six years ago, he relocated to Texas. Within a few weeks, he had landed a job in the Dallas plant's maintenance department. Two years ago, he was promoted to team leader, and last year he became a naturalized American citizen.

While waiting for his dinner at a restaurant on Park City's Main Street, Alex thought about how much he had learned in these first eight weeks in Dallas. He realized, too, that he had a lot more to learn; he had only scratched the surface of what there was to discover about the plant, the people, and the customers. To unlock Dallas's full potential for long-term success and map out an optimal strategic vision for the future, he would have to dig much deeper. Among the team leaders, Lu embodied the insatiable quest for information that separated strategic leaders from merely good managers. The best leaders seem to scan the world around them for new data, constantly refining what they learn as new information comes in. Leaders also kept information continually flowing: communicating, gathering feedback, testing their conclusions, and revising their action plans. Like these strategic thinkers, Lu avidly followed developments that might affect the plant's future and shared what he discovered with his coworkers. As Alex ate, he thought about Lu and what makes him unique.

Lu's information gathering cast a wide net. His interests ranged over local, regional, and international affairs, business and technology, and science. When Alex expressed surprise at how eclectic Lu's interests were, Lu gave credit to his family and his high school history and science teachers. "I was lucky," he said. "I had teachers who were really interested in the world around them, and I've always been curious about how things work." His office shelves were crammed with books, folders, and periodicals, and stacks of titles like *Modern Mechanic* and *Trends* magazine sat on the table behind his desk.

When it came to their own industry, polymer materials and production, Lu was the one person in Dallas who could be depended on to keep up with Jordan when it came to the latest advances in technology and processes. At nearly every daily staff meeting and weekly plant review, he weighed in with ideas for improvements that he had gleaned from his reading, the technical literature that circulated through the plant, information he collected on the web, equipment-vendor seminars he attended, or from his wide network of contacts at other companies. When

Alex noticed Lu had spec sheets for technology that was in use at the Seattle plant but a generation or more ahead of Dallas's equipment, Lu explained, "This is the type of technology we'll need to outperform the competition. I know we've got to get it soon, so I want Maintenance to be ready."

Lu's awareness—of cutting-edge technologies and manufacturing processes—gave him a sense of where the plant needed to go, but not necessarily how it was going to get there. Like most of the staff in Dallas, he was usually too busy dealing with today's problems—or even yesterday's—to look farther out than tomorrow or next week. The aging infrastructure and former management's neglect were partly to blame, but Alex perceived that few of the team leaders were even minimally acquainted with strategy tools or had ever participated in a strategy retreat. They were extremely knowledgeable about the plant's problems and potential, but they didn't look at things through a strategic lens. A few days before Alex's departure from Dallas, Lu told him, "I'm concerned about our future here. I hope you can help us get our bearings." He may not have been aware of it, but he was speaking for the other team leaders as well.

It was no secret that the effort and ingenuity required just to keep the plant running left little time for long-term thinking. In the short time Alex had been in Dallas, production was often hampered or halted because a critical activity or component in the plant broke down. When problems cropped up, Lu was often the key to solving them due to the wealth of information he had at the ready. A few weeks earlier, for example, the entire plant lost power when the main circuit-breaker panel failed. Their electrical-parts supplier told Lu that the panels were no longer being made. Installing a new panel would entail an extensive overhaul, and until that was done, production would be idled.

While Alex and Robert calculated how long it would take to make up for the lost output, Lu was furiously working the phones, calling other suppliers and his counterparts at other plants. An hour later, he contacted a maintenance manager he had met two years earlier at a professional conference; they had struck up a friendship over their shared passion for deep-sea fishing. The friend put him in touch with a parts supplier in Ohio who had the panel they needed and shipped it to Dallas overnight.

This was far from the only time that Lu's pipeline—of people, resources, and information—had bailed the Dallas plant out of a tight spot, but it was one where losing valuable production time would have meant missed delivery dates and threats to quality as Operations attempted to make up for lost time by speeding up production. Whether the problem was with air handlers, production equipment, monitoring systems, or plumbing, Lu always seemed to have the knowledge, a source of information, or a contact who led him to a solution. "You can't panic your way out of a problem," he told Alex, "so you'd better be prepared."

Having good crisis management was important, but avoiding future breakdowns that threatened the plant's viability would be better. And even that was a long way from the strategic acumen that was essential to long-term success. To shift the conversation to the plant's goals for the next 12 months—and ultimately, three or four years beyond that—Alex needed to reframe his team's perspective by introducing them to the principles and thought processes of strategic leaders.

At that stage—to begin early in Phase Two—Lu would be their shining example of leadership awareness, the habit of scanning for data and mining it for the knowledge vital to charting a course for the future. He didn't expect everyone on the team to be masters of Lu's approach, but they would need to get better at watching for signs and signals and using them to extract insights that reveal opportunities, anticipate vulnerabilities, and give them the means to leverage them. Unless leaders are aware of what their customers and competitors are doing and how the world around them is changing, their organizations risk stagnation—or worse, extinction.

We have a long road ahead of us, Alex mused, and it will certainly be an interesting trip. Along the way, Lu would need to learn to be a little less critical of the production staff, whom he was prone to blame when the aging equipment broke down or malfunctioned and his crew was called in to adjust or repair it. Replacing at least some of the oldest equipment would certainly help reduce the friction, but it would be a while before Alex could consider making a case to Melissa and Victor for massive upgrades. Meanwhile, Alex thought, setting Lu up with a coach might help him adopt a more collaborative attitude toward working with Operations, and he would talk to Kim about creating cross-departmental Operations and Maintenance teams to foster better communication and cooperation between the two groups.

From observing Lu in action, Alex also realized that his maintenance manager needed to set better priorities. Good strategy, Alex reminded himself, is all about tradeoffs: knowing what to do and what not to—and when. Scheduling preventive maintenance, for example, would probably boost uptime as much as better training for the technicians. Lu typically worked 60-plus hours a week and usually had too many projects going on concurrently. As a result, he sometimes relied on his team members to see the work through to completion, but then didn't exercise sufficient oversight to ensure that they followed through. Alex suspected that was what had caused recent incidents on the production floor, as when a ladder Maintenance had carelessly left in a precarious spot fell over and damaged a piece of equipment nearby. He was determined to spread Lu's extraordinary talents across the entire team. In exchange, he would work with his maintenance manager to set priorities and focus on them, the way Robert consistently kept his eye on the plant's production targets.

Alex had gotten so absorbed in pondering Lu's uncanny ability to gather invaluable information that he hadn't noticed that his check was waiting for him on the table. He wouldn't reach his destination—Hood River, Oregon, where he planned to spend the night—until late, but he was determined to be at the Columbia River Gorge early the next morning. Before getting on the road, he checked in with the plant and called Julie to let her know that with a little luck, he'd be home the next day, and then he headed to his car, ready to travel on.

Awareness Close-Up

One of the pillars of strategic leadership is something we call awareness. In this context, awareness is the strategic leader's ability to gather information that they can use to develop a full picture of the world in which they operate. Strategic leaders with high levels of awareness pay attention to the road signs and indicators that will influence their future so they can act on their insights. They recognize that by being attuned to all kinds of signals, they have greater control over the forces that will shape their future—forces that can either work for them or against them. This information helps them form a point of view about their current situation and the opportunities and challenges they see on the horizon. In comparison, leaders who are consumed by daily demands (or are simply less attentive to the world around them) are often exposed to unwelcome surprises and are much more likely to miss windows of opportunities that open up. Strategic awareness isn't just about seeing and understanding information, data, and signs, but about figuring out how to take action on that information in order to achieve better results and contribute to the organization's core strategy and mission. So what, exactly, does an alert and aware leader do to increase his or her personal level of strategic awareness and gain these valuable insights? Let's take a closer look at the four main elements of strategic awareness.

1. Exercising Discipline

Leaders with high strategic awareness have the discipline needed to pause and move away from the activity magnet that exercises a powerful grip on many leaders' lives. We call it taming the beast. As leaders, many of us have been programmed to think fast, take quick action, and be doers, fixers, and problem-solvers. This isn't an altogether bad thing. We certainly need the ability to take quick action and rapidly resolve issues in many situations. The caution is this: Any strength that is overused or carried to an extreme can really hurt you in the long run. A lot of leaders are addicted to activity. People like getting things done. But when this preference is carried to excess, the urge to focus on short-term priorities, or the tyranny of the urgent, puts your long-term success at risk.

On the other hand, when strategic leaders have the discipline to step back from the day-to-day firefighting and engage in break-through thinking, they are able to really see things of longer-term significance that give them a better perspective on their world. This can be quite refreshing, and you'll be surprised at what you'll see and discover when you detach yourself from the daily grind. We aren't suggesting that you should fail to meet your normal obligations at work—not in the least. It's important to fulfill your typical daily responsibilities and expectations, but to do so in a balanced way. In the *Harvard Business Review* (May, 2010) article entitled "Need Speed? Slow Down" by Jocelyn R. Davis and Tom Atkinson, they describe a study they conducted on the differences between strategically fast companies and strategically slow ones. Their study indicated that the "firms that 'slowed down to speed up'" were able to greatly improve both their sales and their profits, averaging 40 percent higher sales and 52 percent higher operating profits over three years. They also found that people in strategically slow companies don't take time to reflect. On the other hand, higher-performing companies with strategic speed did allow time for reflection and learning. The lesson is this: Don't sacrifice the time you could be using to work on strategic endeavors just so you can deal with daily distractions. Remember that busy doesn't always mean productive. Cut yourself off from the constant pump of adrenaline, the high that comes from constant activity. Instead of being busy for busy's sake, work to conserve some of your time, resources, and energy and use it to fulfill your responsibilities as a shaper of the future.

We're serious about this. Set aside a little time each day, week, or month to get away from your routine demands and the flood of electronic messages that consume so much of our time. When he was CEO at Microsoft, Bill Gates had his own way of doing this. He called it "Think Week," a seven-day period during which he went into seclusion and thought about the future. A seven-day stretch may not be realistic for you, but setting a regular strategic meeting with yourself, even a short one, will help you step back and broaden your view of the horizon. Drawing this line can be hard—even for people with the very best intentions—but it has to be done. You need to be respectful of that strategic space, and you have to teach others to be respectful of it, too. And on days when it's especially challenging to find that time, remind yourself that you can't really claim to be adding your full value to the organization if your focus is placed squarely on the things that are happening in front of you right now.

2. Gathering Information

After strategic leaders slow themselves down and break free from the activity trap, they focus on building up their base of information and knowledge. Information is the lifeblood of strategy. In a lot of ways, strategic information is like oxygen: It is all around us, and all we have to do is breathe it in and process it. But when it comes to information, some people are better at finding and absorbing it than others. In addition, sometimes information is pure and other times it can be polluted, just like oxygen. Strategic leaders hunt for the clear air—trustworthy, relevant information—by tracking valuable sources of intelligence and making sense of what it means for them and their team.

Awareness provides the strategic leader with indicators of where to go to create value for the organization, what hazards to avoid, and which resources to leverage down the road. Think of it as mental radar that sweeps continuously across the spectrum of your world. Your world, or dashboard, might include your team, processes, resources, functional area, organization, industry, market, customers, technology, and so on. This dashboard is where you search for ideas and opportunities and spot potential threats. The strategic signals, direction, and priorities of the broader organization comprise one of the most important streams of information you'll want to track. Gathering information in this area will give you clues about how to align your strategic efforts to the overarching strategic direction of the business. Here are a few things you need to consider and attend to if you haven't already.

1. The organization's needs and direction, whether they have been explicitly stated or not.
2. The current and emerging needs of your internal and/or external customers. You and your team are closest to the customer and are in the best position to know what their expectations and needs are.
3. The forces and dynamics outside of your team that can have a huge impact—positive and negative—on your goals. The key is to look at the truly relevant, specific factors in the internal and external environment that could affect you, not just broad generalizations, ambiguous trends, or worst-case scenarios.

A simple way to get started is to make a list of the really important variables or elements of your operating environment that have the potential to influence the future success of your team and the organization. For example, if you are a supply-chain manager, you might need to monitor the price of raw materials. For a human-resources manager, it might be changes in the labor market. If you are a maintenance manager, maybe it's a new generation of tools. If you are in sales, it could be a competitor's newest promotion designed to cut into your customer base. Once you know which key areas you should keep your eye on, you can begin building a process that will help you stay abreast of the signals and information that are priorities for you.

We now have access to more information than we could ever realistically hope to use thanks, in part, to mind-bending advances in technology. Information comes to us in a constant stream.

This can be both good and bad. With so much information at our disposal, sifting through the clutter to find what is truly meaningful to us can be quite daunting. Collecting too much information can be very costly in terms of your time and resources, so look for ways to strike a balance between having too much information and having too little. Make sure you gather enough data that you can form insights and make educated decisions, but don't collect so much that you're overwhelmed by the volume—or so little that it would create blind spots as you move forward.

Take some time to do your homework. Be attentive and connected to what is going on around you so you can be smart about the future. Trying to monitor everything isn't necessary (or plausible), but don't be oblivious to the road signs that are out there, either.

3. Inferring Meaning

A strategic leader is good at amassing and compiling pieces of information, to be sure, but it doesn't end there. Noted astronomer and author Dr. Carl Sagan said, " . . . intelligence is not information alone but also judgment, the manner in which information is collected and used." Once strategic leaders gather the information they need, they must screen it, make connections, and translate all of what they have learned into a meaningful message. They build their understanding of the future by seeking an answer to a question: What is the information telling me, and what does it *mean*? This is the point where you will be able to pick up on the emerging opportunities and spot storms on the horizon. Some information will be irrelevant; some might even be inaccurate or misleading. This means you'll need to be willing to do a little sorting and sifting. And even then, strategic leaders often have to place an educated bet in order to get traction and make a strategic move.

Sometimes the information you gather may not seem pertinent or valuable at first, but you never know: somewhere farther down the road, that useless information might actually become very useful after all. Looking for clues and connecting the dots reveals what you can expect to encounter. This will help you follow a path or create an entirely new path that will allow you to reach your long-term objectives.

As you make observations and mine your data, you will begin to uncover the guiding principles, essential rules, or natural patterns that govern how things work in your business. Stay attuned to the indicators, trends, correlations, and root causes you see. This will help you decipher the codes and patterns around you. The data reveals—and also conceals—insights and discoveries about the environment you have to navigate as you pursue your strategic objectives. It helps you be proactive as you work toward achieving your goals and allows you to better anticipate threats and hazards. Finally, increasing your situational awareness helps you prepare for challenges and recognize windows of opportunity.

When needed, reach out to your network of advisors and mentors. They may be able to help you make sense of what you see or provide answers to questions you have. Talking with others will usually give you a richer perspective and some alternatives to consider. As you tune in to your environment and translate the information and clues it offers, you need to be willing to consider the realities of the situation—even when they're harsh. Studies have shown that leaders frequently overestimate the positive conditions and underestimate the challenges that lie ahead. Great strategic leaders work hard to gain a complete and honest picture of their situation, regardless of whether the information is positive or negative in nature.

The awareness engines of strategic leaders are always running. These leaders are curious, and they work hard to interpret what they see. When you are informed and aware, you are able to turn information into knowledge, knowledge into decisions, and decisions into actions. That is what organizations want from their trusted leaders at every level.

4. *Taking Intelligent Action*

The final component of strategic awareness is having the ability not only to recognize the implications and meaning of the information you gather, but to convert that recognition into action. Ask yourself what the patterns suggest in terms of new options and actions you could take. The answer to that question will allow you to formulate some plausible potential scenarios that could unfold and help you understand the choices that lie before you. You won't be able to predict what's ahead with absolute certainty, but you can anticipate likely events and outcomes and be better prepared. This will help you pay close attention to what matters most and keep you on track so you don't overlook or dismiss any important indicators or variables. Be mindful of the fact that you aren't just preparing for the worst-case scenario; you also need to think about how you might seize opportunities or turn potentially adverse issues into rewarding possibilities.

What It All Means

The bottom line is this: For you to achieve leadership excellence, you have to be able to create some space for yourself to think strategically and step back from the action from time to time. Raise your level of awareness by looking for (and really seeing) the harbingers and signals, making sense of the raw data, and forming some conclusions. Taking a breather from the typical "Go, go, go!" mentality will allow you to really see the big picture. Give yourself a chance to identify and diagnose strategic opportunities, threats, and issues so you can explore creative options and choose the best solutions for taking on the future in a meaningful way. Some of the most significant strategic moves, improvements, or breakthroughs are the result of everyday discoveries.

As a strategic leader, the most important asset you have is information. Don't insulate yourself. Keep your eyes and ears open as you hunt for potential threats and promising opportunities. In many ways, strategic awareness truly is a paradox: It requires you to pause before moving forward. Before you put the pedal to the metal, give yourself the time to idle, check the road signs, and get a sense of where you're going. Doing so allows you to see new pathways and patterns that keep you on the road to success and allow you to achieve better outcomes for all of your stakeholders. Our ability to think gives us nearly unlimited potential; all we have to do is use the power of our own genius to harness the information that's out there and make it work for us.

11

The Art of Driving Change

The Story: Sara

At 6 A.M., Alex bounded out of bed, threw on his biking gear, and hurried over to a local café for breakfast. At that early hour, only a few other customers were in the restaurant. All were dressed, as he was, for hiking or bicycling. Before setting out for his ride along the Columbia River, he checked his email, a task he deferred during yesterday's long drive.

On this sunny morning, Alex was excited to be back at the Columbia River Gorge, but his feelings were also tinged with regret. The Gorge was one of his favorite areas in the Pacific Northwest, and at just a three-hour drive from Seattle, he had made dozens of trips here over the years to camp, hike, and bike. Today he felt almost as if he had come to say goodbye to an old friend. Shrugging off his melancholy, he reminded himself that change, especially because it held the possibility of great rewards for the Dallas plant, would inevitably be disruptive. Leaving Seattle was turning out to be more difficult than he'd expected it to be, but taking the Dallas offer had been the right move. Dallas was his shot at navigating around the obstacles to advancement, opening up exciting new possibilities to grow, and putting his new plant at the center of the company's blueprint for the future.

The team leaders in Dallas gave Alex ample grounds for optimism; over the course of his first eight weeks at the plant, he'd discovered that they were even more resourceful, creative, and forward-looking than he and Victor had judged them to be prior to the PSI acquisition. Some were diamonds in the rough, to be sure. But others, especially Sara, the controller, had little difficulty balancing their day-to-day responsibilities with a focus on the plant's long-term goals. Like Alex, Sara was a transplant to Dallas; Sara had transferred from the Chicago plant two years prior to PSI's recent acquisition. Also like Alex, she made the move because there were too many people ahead of her in the queue for senior leadership positions. If she had remained in Chicago, she might have had to wait 10 years or more—until the plant controller retired or moved on—to advance her career.

As he pedaled east from the trailhead in Hood River, Alex was following the route of the original Columbia River Highway, now converted into biking and hiking trails. He rode at a leisurely pace along the forested paths and past the sheer basalt cliffs, enjoying the crisp early-morning air. In the clearings, he had views of the river and some of the more than 100 waterfalls that cascade down the sides of the Gorge, fed by mountain streams that empty into the river and its tributaries.

Along the length of the Gorge, the terrain varies from fertile forests and farms to semi-arid land and is home to some four dozen vineyards and hundreds of orchards that grow apples, cherries, and pears. As the heart of this vast ecosystem, the Columbia River also provides spawning grounds for sturgeon and several varieties of salmon, water for agricultural irrigation, and hydroelectric power from a series of dams that stretch from Canada to the Pacific Ocean. The river is truly instrumental to life in this area.

On a smaller scale, Alex reflected, Sara's role at the Dallas plant resembled that of the river in the Pacific Northwest. Her fiscal stewardship sustained the activities of every phase of the business, from sales through shipping. In fact, in addition to being the plant controller, she had responsibility for raw materials procurement, warehousing, and shipping. Because Sara kept tabs on every department's share of the overall budget, her colleagues took her recommendations about where to gain efficiencies and where to make long-term investments very seriously. As a result, she had also become an influential voice and advocate for change at the plant.

In her chief role, she compiled the plant's key performance indicators (KPIs) and charted its bottom-line results, the measurements on which senior management based its assessment of Dallas's contribution to the corporate balance sheet and the satisfaction of its customers. Even at this early stage, Alex foresaw that it might be advantageous to split off management of the supply chain, warehouse, and shipping functions from Sara's controller responsibilities. This would enable her to provide more advisory services to her colleagues down the line, but for the moment, the plant benefited from her end-to-end view of everything that happened at the plant.

Like Kim, the head of HR, Sara is the leader of a team that provides services to internal customers; she has no direct involvement in the finished products manufactured at the plant. In a workplace where drama is almost a daily occurrence, no one was entirely above the fray, but her distance from some of the day-to-day turmoil and pressures afforded her a degree of objectivity. That distance is critical, because Alex expected Sara to be at the epicenter of the revolution that was about to unfold in Dallas.

On her own, she'd already taken steps in that direction. Shortly before Alex's arrival, she introduced a visual management system (VMS) for materials procurement and warehousing that eliminated the pattern of under- and overstock, as well as lost, misplaced, and delayed items that increased costs and hampered production. Since then, she shared many ideas with Alex that were geared to making Dallas more nimble, more progressive, and more profitable.

Sara's proposals and innovations would pay for themselves over time, Alex knew. One idea she shared with Alex during his first weeks in Dallas was a new tracking and scanning system for the production floor. After only a brief discussion, Maintenance and Operations bought in to the idea, formed a task force, and started to experiment and test out various ideas. In the first month alone, key metrics started to improve in a significant way. More recently, she suggested repurposing funds from the maintenance budget to upgrade equipment and technology by purchasing newer, refurbished equipment. That proposal, which would require Victor's approval, was still under discussion—but her business case indicated that making this investment would boost the plant's output by a double-digit factor.

"I never expected to leave Chicago," Sara told Alex when they compared notes about moving to Dallas. "I grew up in Rockford and went to college and business school at the University of Illinois in Champaign–Urbana, and when I first got my MBA, I would only interview for jobs in Chicago." Almost all of her friends were there, and she loved the city's cultural and ethnic diversity, its theater, and its nightlife. Even after two years in Dallas, Sara, who was unattached, went back as regularly as one weekend a month, often just to hang out with friends.

Sara's social circle in Chicago, Alex knew, included her former colleagues at the Chicago plant, and Alex knew it was inevitable that they engaged in shop talk. Alex continued to do the same with his PSI colleagues in Seattle. He was also certain that Sara had figured out that PSI might consider disposing of one of its two newly acquired plants at some point in the future. The intention hadn't been formally announced, but any controller or plant manager as savvy as Sara could read the corporate business plan, growth forecasts, and capacity and capital-expenditure projections that were periodically issued from headquarters and see the writing on the wall. Alex was certain that she had mixed emotions about the competition playing out between Dallas and Chicago. Alex knew he would feel the same way if Seattle were Dallas's adversary in a contest for survival, and Sara was cautious about sharing the details of Chicago's progress and pitfalls. Alex didn't doubt, however, that her loyalties lay with Dallas. Like him, Sara didn't like to lose; she hadn't uprooted herself from her beloved city only to have her career dead-end in Dallas.

From PSI's perspective, fueling a not-so-subtle competition between Dallas and Chicago made perfect sense: It would spur the Chicago and Dallas teams to pull out all the stops to show the home office their capacity to deliver short-term results and simultaneously roll out a strategy for long-term, sustained growth.

When Alex emerged from one of a pair of tunnels cut through a section of rock when the Columbia River Highway was built in 1921, the sun was already high in the sky. It would be a hot day, but at the moment a strong breeze coming off the river almost hinted at fall. Weather at the Gorge was notoriously fickle, and there was a chance of high winds in any season. Undeterred, Alex kept going, climbing hills that passed orchards and dropping down to thread his way through sheer canyons before coasting to the eastern end of the trail.

On this first leg of his ride, the wind had been at Alex's back; on the return he would be pedaling into the wind. A strong cyclist, he was undeterred. As he started back toward Hood River, he reflected on Sara's readiness to move forward no matter how resistant the corporate winds might be. That was one reason he quietly referred to her as a change driver rather than using the more conventional term change agent. Although she hadn't articulated an overarching plan for Dallas's future—and hadn't yet had time to learn much about PSI's long-term corporate vision—her valuable insights and innovative ideas frequently had a strategic cast to them. Just as important, she looked at every process with the intent of changing it for the better, and she never hesitated to challenge the status quo if it stood in the way of creating greater value, reducing bureaucracy, or simplifying the business. She liked to say, "It's better to ask for forgiveness than permission." Whether an idea involved her own team, another department, or a supplier, when Sara saw a way to improve the plant's performance, she explained the issues, listened to the arguments on both sides, and then pressed for buy-in and adoption of best practices that would strengthen the plant's position. She backed up her impassioned arguments with hard statistics and evidence, and these were usually enough to convince even her most cautious colleagues, especially now that everyone was aware that Dallas had to reinvent itself and earn a place in the PSI family.

To Alex, Sara's status as change driver meant that her initiatives also inspired others to think about making strategic contributions of their own. That hadn't happened often yet, but Alex was confident that her spirit would soon catch on. Sara's example was already beginning to embolden him to think big and go all in with his ideas. He had no doubt that with just a bit of encouragement, others would get on board.

As Alex ascended a hill and saw Hood River spread out just below, he suddenly realized that for the past several miles, he had been thinking so intently about Dallas that he'd paid almost no attention to the mighty river flowing just below the trail. He wasn't even in Seattle yet, but already he was impatient to return to Dallas, get back in the fight, and find a way to win. Fifteen minutes later, he was in his hotel room, where he showered and changed before grabbing a quick lunch and pointing his car toward home. He called Julie from the road. "I'll be home by dinnertime. Make a reservation at one of our favorite restaurants. Tonight, we're going to celebrate."

Driving Change Close-Up

In this market-driven, competitive world, organizations that want to be relevant in the future have no choice but to change and evolve. Experts agree that the pace of change will continue to accelerate over time. So what are the implications for you and your team? It means that as a leader, you will need to do things that are different from the things you may have done in the past. You won't be able to conduct business as usual. You'll have to tear down ingrained habits and old standards in order to rebuild something stronger and better. You won't be able to afford to wait for pain points and issues to surface—and you definitely can't let things outlive their useful lives. In order to prevent your team or organization from fading into obsolescence, you have to be at the forefront of change and take action on new ideas and windows of opportunity as they open up. This means having the drive and sheer will necessary to challenge the status quo. It means coming up with new, breakthrough ideas about how to capture future opportunities, not just solve today's problems. In short, it means you have to be a change driver.

Perspectives on Change

Two types of change occur in organizations: change that is driven by someone or something and change that occurs naturally. Driven change is deliberate and designed with a specific purpose in mind and is an important part of strategic leadership. The catalyst for this type of change can be forces that are either internal or external, and sometimes they are both. Change that is intentional is important because it puts us in the driver's seat as we work to shape the future, capitalize on opportunities, and proactively address issues that are potential roadblocks. Strategic leaders are "change drivers" for two reasons: (1) They see the need for change and (2) they work hard to push the needed change forward. Both components are necessary. The power of the change driver is not just his or her ability to proactively see and understand the changes that are needed, but to intervene and take action in order to achieve better results for the organization.

In business, as in life, there is a tendency to avoid fixing things that aren't, technically, broken. The rationale is often, "Why go to the effort of doing something different if what we're doing now seems to be working pretty well? At least we know what the outcome is going to be." This point of view underscores a common, but significant, difference in leaders' outlooks on the future. Many leaders can't overcome the pressure to conform or will settle for good enough because they know how difficult instituting organizational change can be. Forward-thinking leaders, on the other hand, seek out and drive change deliberately because at their core, they have a deep desire to make things better. True, change can cause create a lot of discomfort. As humans, we are wired to seek pleasure and avoid pain. It's part of our DNA. We are biologically attracted to self-preservation. So the fact that many of us avoid the pain of change at all costs makes a lot of sense—sort of. The problem with avoiding the discomfort associated with change is that we aren't forced to grow, improve, evolve, or adapt. And when that happens—well, we leaders and our organizations may end up going the proverbial way of the dinosaurs.

Some leaders are better equipped to manage change with ease and resiliency than others. You can probably relate to the variety of reactions you see in people who are dealing with change. Generally speaking, we have found that people approach change in one of three ways: They will either be change-averse, change-tolerant, or change-seeking. As you read more about these three styles, think about your own inclinations when you encounter change.

1. Change-averse individuals prefer current conditions to the unknown. They tend to be regimented, detail-oriented, and organized. They prefer steady, stable, and structured environments and they feel much more comfortable adhering to existing rules and regulations than challenging the status quo. At best, they favor change that is gradual, incremental, and maintains the current structure. They solve problems or address issues in ways that are familiar to them and gravitate toward tested or proven solutions.

2. Change-tolerant individuals are primarily interested in what will work best in a given situation, so they tend to be reasonable, flexible, and agreeable. They are usually team-oriented and prefer change that reflects the needs and demands of the current circumstances. You will often find that change-tolerant individuals act as mediators between individuals who are change-averse and those who seek change because they can see both sides of the argument. They typically solve problems by taking a middle-of-the-road approach, but they are happy to challenge the status quo if it keeps them from making progress toward a more productive outcome.

3. Change-seeking individuals prefer expansive and significant change that occurs quickly. Others may see them as disorganized, unconventional, spontaneous, and impulsive. They are comfortable challenging conventional wisdom as well as

existing practices and thinking in order to make sweeping, fundamental changes. Change-seeking individuals are often seen as visionaries and are usually quite innovative. Others may interpret their behavior as being dismissive of existing policies or rules. Change seekers look for new ways to complete a job and may focus more on new ideas and innovation than on relationships and team cohesiveness.

If developing the qualities of a change driver is something you need to work on, having a sense of your natural inclinations when it comes to change will give you some insights and the greater self-awareness needed to stretch your abilities. As you think about these three perspectives toward change, recognize that we all have different personalities and experiences that shape our style or outlook. Having people on your team who have very different perspectives on change is actually a good thing because it provides balance and allows you to make better decisions about change. However, as a leader, being a change driver is central to everything we do and is critical to making a strategic difference. Because having the ability to push strategic change forward is so crucial in a leadership role, it is particularly important for us leaders to be aware of our tendencies and preferences so we can expand our ability to drive change rather than simply reacting to it.

The Quest for Change

Strategic leaders don't wait to be caught off guard by a critical turning point that suddenly appears. Instead, they monitor critical signals to anticipate changes on the horizon or detect a change they can champion. They build a culture where ingrained patterns and routines are broken down and boundaries are redefined in a positive way. These leaders refuse to wait for things to happen to them. They don't necessarily have to be riddled with discomfort, problems, or organizational pain to know that a change is needed. They know that there are opportunities out there that they can act on proactively, and they're on the hunt. Based on what they see, sense, and understand about their Business-within-the Business, change drivers instinctively know that they need to do something new, take some kind of strategic action, and introduce a change (or series of changes) in order to get the organization into a better position. Leaders who are not natural change drivers often have great ideas that offer potential value to the organization, but they don't drive those changes forward. They may not feel that proposing change is their role. Perhaps they encounter self-doubt. Maybe they talk themselves out of taking action and making an investment that could lead to positive results. It's even possible that they may be somewhat averse to change by nature, and as a result, they shy away from upsetting the routine or status quo. Some people struggle with taking proactive action on a strategic change initiative because they know it will entail extra work. For others, the challenge is learning to recognize and control the inner critic. Whatever it may be that stands in your way, focus on cultivating your inner motivation to achieve your goals and get positioned for the future. Pay attention to your thought processes. Coach yourself to get out of your routine and try something new—*anything* new. Challenge yourself to work outside your comfort zone and look at it as an opportunity to grow. Change drivers remind themselves that the change process always begins imperfectly. As with taking a risk, when driving needed change, you have to give yourself permission to experiment, fail, learn from the experience, and move on. Stumbling a bit is just part of the process.

You are likely to find many avenues to pursue, but try to look for the change opportunities that allow you to have the greatest impact. If you don't like where things are going or what is happening right now, change what you are doing. You can make a difference if you find the courage and take the first step.

Uncovering the Innovative Possibilities

Change drivers have an innovative spark. They are imaginative and look for novel or unusual ideas, not just those that are obvious. A good change driver doesn't have to be a genius or especially creative, but they are always asking, "Is there a better way?" They open their minds to the possibilities and are willing to experiment. They notice things around them and make connections between what they perceive and the strategic opportunities they see or the problems they want to solve. Joel Barker, a futurist, calls this the Verge. According to Barker, the Verge is where differences come together to trigger new ideas or new combinations. Change drivers, like Sara, aren't afraid of looking for new ways to connect diverse ideas and come up with new and unexpected solutions.

For many of us, the creative process is delicate. When you run into a creative block or go through a creative slowdown, you have to be patient with yourself. Engage your team or other colleagues in a brainstorming session. This will help you prime the pump and stimulate some fresh ideas about what or how to change. Ideas themselves are a dime a dozen. So, once you see an idea that has real potential, you need to shift into a can-do mentality and explore the idea's possibilities. Normally, one idea will lead to another until you have something more significant. It may even become a game changer. Don't lose interest or momentum in the early stages of the ideation phase. Give your innovative idea a chance to gain some traction and invite others to get involved. This will help sustain you in the fragile initial stages of the change process. Change drivers rarely have a detailed plan for the change early on, so they are willing to go with the flow and figure out how things might come together. They trust their instincts and let each step unfold naturally, but with the end in mind. Remember that ideas are translated into innovative change by taking action.

On those occasions when you run into what seems like an insurmountable obstacle, take a break, step back, and rethink the process. Everyone is bound to get stuck on occasion, including change drivers. Again, learn to control your inner critic. Ignore the voice that says "you don't have good ideas" or "that change will be much too hard to execute." Fifteen hundred CEOs who were interviewed for the IBM Global CEO study reported that creativity is the single, most-important leadership competency. Senior leaders know that innovation is important. Just imagine the exciting possibilities that are available to you when you let your creativity and ideas flow.

Getting Buy-In

As a change driver, you need to make a compelling case for the changes you propose and help others understand the necessity and value of those changes. Strategic change requires that you enroll others in the process, so it's imperative for you to help people understand that the cost and pain of change outweighs the costs of staying the current course and doing nothing. Guide people toward an understanding that ultimately, the change will create a better reality for everyone. Chances are good that you will experience some resistance to the changes you propose. If you're lucky, you won't have a team full of change-averse people to contend with. Still, everyone will be better off if you review why the change is necessary and the rationale behind the shift. People need to grasp where you are now, the circumstances that led to the current state, where you are trying to go, and how the change will get you there. Provide details, evidence, background information, and as much context as you can, and give people plenty of opportunities to ask questions and discuss their concerns in an open forum. A recent study we conducted with a global manufacturing company found that a lack of communication was the number-one obstacle in the way of implementing vital initiatives and priorities successfully. This example underscores how imperative it is to maintain open lines of communication prior to the change, as well as during its implementation. Doing so helps people see your personal commitment and optimism about the results that the change will help you achieve as a team. Sometimes even the strongest adversaries are swayed by the passion of others and knowing that they won't have to weather the change on their own.

Making It Happen

If you are not a change seeker by nature but can see the value of change, be mindful of the common pitfalls that follow.

- Being overly critical or judgmental of new ideas.
- Being close-minded about a variety of creative possibilities.
- Fearing ambiguity and uncertainty about a different approach.
- Being unwilling to question ideas, accepted practices, and norms.
- Spending too little (or no) time looking for innovative patterns and combinations.
- Being unwilling or unable to allocate the time and energy to more complex change.
- Having a negative perception about change based on past experiences.

Obstacles like these may be preventing you from driving change in your organization that will get you to a better place, but if you can see them for what they are and work to overcome them, you'll be in a much stronger position to become the change driver you want to be.

People are better able to drive change when they have the discipline to work *on* the business instead of working solely *in* the business. The fundamental idea is this: Play to your strengths when driving change—both your personal strengths and those of your team members. You don't have to try to change everything at once. Don't try to swim against the tide all the time; take advantage of the pull and power of the water. See whether there are ways to get where you want to go by working with and capitalizing on the strengths of your organization's culture. Which existing processes and practices could you reinvent or rework? You cannot see yourself simply as someone who implements change provided by authorities above if you truly want to be a driver of change.

Implementing top–down change is important, but you also have to recognize and initiate productive and innovative change yourself. You have to do the work to transform your piece of the business and ultimately help the organization get better. This is needed change that only you will recognize. Keep in mind that without change, you will be unable to progress as an organization—and that although change may be hard, standing idly by while you become obsolete is much, much harder.

12 | The Art of Vision

The Story: Alex

Alex's last week in Seattle was a dizzying round of dinners and backyard barbecues, where he, Julie, and the boys said goodbye to friends, colleagues, and family, and a seemingly endless chain of errands and packing in preparation for their new life in Texas. Only a few days after Alex got back, the family—with the help of a moving company—had their furniture, clothing, and personal effects loaded into the van that would arrive in Dallas the day their flight landed. It was a lot of work, but Alex was energized after taking a few days to himself on the road.

After the moving van was loaded, the family stayed with Julie's parents, who still lived in the large Mercer Island house where she had grown up. The entire family was thrilled to have a few more days together before moving halfway across the country. Throughout these few days, Alex slipped back into a purely tactical, problem-solving mode. He had always been able to switch almost instantaneously between the big picture and close-up modes of thinking, zooming in and out like a camera lens, in response to whatever a given situation demanded.

Alex understood why solving problems was so appealing. The rush of adrenaline that often accompanied the unknotting of even a relatively minor problem could be addictive. Over the years, Alex had come to describe the attraction as "the task magnet," the pull of getting things done and wanting to be the hero who saves the day. Leading a business team often demanded heroics of that sort, but Alex knew that in Dallas, he had to rise above the fray and keep his eye on where he wanted the plant to be three years from now, or even farther out. No matter how pressing the daily crises were or how precarious the plant's viability seemed, his role as leader was to chart a course that would lead to a prosperous future. No one wanted to be on the losing side of even a minor altercation, yet there are no rewards for heroes who win every battle but ultimately lose the war.

Alex had worked for managers who got stuck dealing with immediate issues and never got past that stage. It seemed that they were doomed never to elevate their organizations to new levels of performance or prepare for the future. He wasn't going to fall into that trap. In fact, he was sure that one reason he had been selected to manage one of PSI's two newly acquired plants was his zoom-lens dexterity, his ability to straddle the invisible line between short- and long-term business needs. With his Dallas team, Alex knew that he would be creating a new paradigm, showing them how to incorporate strategic thinking into daily activities, switch between short- and long-term perspectives as needed, cultivate their current leadership qualities, and discover how to develop new ones. Occasionally, a team leader—or even another employee—would ask Alex where he thought the plant was headed, but he wanted them to evolve from merely posing questions to proposing their own answers. There would be a steep learning curve. They had never before been asked to contribute to a strategic plan of any kind, let alone being asked to create their own strategy that was linked and aligned with the business; the previous management had confined the team leader's roles to attacking the pressing problems of the moment, leaving it to others to worry about strategy. That was a mistake; strategy was everybody's business at every level of the organization.

At Sea-Tac Airport, the entire family was in a state of high excitement, although Julie worried about whether she would have time to get everyone settled into their rental house before the first day of new-teacher orientation at the Dallas magnet high school for the sciences where she had been hired. Alex couldn't wait to get started on Phase Two at the plant. As soon as they had settled into their seats he began to review the highlights of the last two months and his action plan for the initial stage of Phase Two. He liked the qualities his core team of leaders had revealed so far, and now he wondered what they expected from him. Did he have a unique talent to add to the mix, like Kim's agility, for example, or Jordan's shrewd risk-taking?

Alex looked across at Michael, who was absorbed in the drawing he was creating on his tablet. Not so different from what I'm doing, he thought, using tools to visualize something that doesn't yet exist. Alex didn't think of himself as a visionary thinker, but he admitted that he was creating a vision of the Dallas plant three to five years from now, assisted by contributions from his talented team and constrained by budgetary limitations, the ability to penetrate new markets and manufacture innovative products, the state of the economy, and other factors. It was essential that the vision be collaborative, and he was eager to share the credit, but he knew he would have to lead the process.

Alex saw that the seatbelt sign was flashing and heard the pilot announce that they were about to push back from the gate and would be taking off soon. A few minutes later, the plane was in the air, and a picture of Dallas's future was taking shape in Alex's mind. He saw a large, new, state-of-the-art plant on the 15-acre plot adjoining the current building. Inside, the production floor was humming with the latest equipment, turning out advanced components and monitored in real time by fully integrated technology. He also saw Robert and some of his staff touring the plant with groups of customers, and other clients conferring about specs with Jordan or one of his staff engineers or discussing orders with the sales and business-development reps who ministered to Dallas's growing roster of domestic and international customers and prospects.

When they reached cruising altitude, Alex quickly pulled out his own tablet. He wanted to get his recent thoughts down and share them with the team. After all, he thought, why not communicate a bird's-eye vision of the world from 35,000 feet? Thirty minutes later, he had composed an outline of his approach and a first pass at a vision statement.

Team,

Needless to say, I am very excited about the future opportunities and potential of PSI's Dallas plant. I am sharing my thoughts with you now because I want you to share your vision of our future and your ideas about how we can reach the next level of performance, customer share, innovation, and growth. A vision will help the entire organization, at every level, get a better sense of what our direction and strategy are. A vision is like a GPS; it helps us get our bearings, but it's up to us to reach our destination. It's not a catalog of key objectives, list of initiatives, or plan of action. It's a concise picture of what we want our organization to be in the future.

I know that the draft of the vision statement I've included below is just that—a draft. As such, I have no pride of authorship in this first pass. I am sharing my initial thoughts for our vision statement simply to spur your thinking and start the conversation. Please share your comments, propose changes to any part of what I've written, or feel free to create your own completely independent picture.

Vision Statement (1st draft):

We have a vision of PSI's Dallas Plant—significantly larger than today—focused on new, essential devices, some based on cutting-edge composite materials, as well as our traditional line of high-performance, polymer-based products. We will be known for our speed in adopting new customer programs and delivering on schedule. We will have a highly energized and engaged workforce, thoroughly trained, innovative, and committed to PSI for the long term. New, old, and prospective customers will line up to visit our facility, eager to make us their preferred supplier and curious about how we produce our extraordinarily high-quality products at competitive prices. We will be an aligned and forward-focused leadership team that delivers superior bottom-line performance. Shareholders will delight in the value we create and their return on investment. Suppliers will work with us like partners, and competitors will struggle to match our cutting-edge business model and strategy.

Let's plan to discuss everyone's thoughts at our team's quarterly strategy retreat next week. I am looking forward to being back at the plant tomorrow.

Alex

In sharing his vision with the team even before returning to Dallas, Alex's intention was to urge them to respond and start a conversation about their goals for the next three to five years. In the process, the individual team leaders would have to devise their own personal strategic plans and align them with the broader shared vision. The exercise would heighten their awareness of their own strategic strengths and clarify why they needed to broaden their skillsets as well.

At cruising altitude, Alex remembered, it could be easy to lose track of the possible pitfalls and to imagine that potential obstacles were as easy to spot—and to circumvent—on the ground as storms on a radar screen. Just then, he felt the plane shudder slightly and out the window, he saw lightning flashes to the west of their flight path. Instinctively, he checked his family's seatbelts, then reflected on how unreliable forecasts often were in an industry that was changing as rapidly as this one. The market shifted constantly, as new businesses with unprecedented needs came online, and older ones faded away. Competitors often sprang up like mushrooms after a rainstorm, challenging even established players with aggressive pricing and sales tactics. New technologies, materials, and processes continually cropped up, and a company that made a few poor predictions could discover that it had been left behind. Some—or even all—of those obstacles might threaten to derail his plans for Dallas, but Alex had confidence in his team and his own ability to anticipate trends. They would take risks, but calculated ones; they would keep close watch on the market, on the competition, and on technological advances; they would be nimble and agile, correcting course when changing conditions demanded it. That's what strategic vision was all about, he thought, just as the pilot announced that they were beginning their descent into Dallas. "We're almost home," he whispered to himself, and thought, *It's time to get my feet back on the ground.*

Vision Close-Up

After studying, writing, and teaching about strategic thinking and leadership for many years, we have discovered that vision is at the very center of successful strategic leadership. Visionary leaders, like Alex, know exactly what winning means for them, their teams, and the organization. They know what they want and can see it, crystal clear, in their mind's eye. They can picture themselves and their teams getting to a better place and achieving the outcomes they desire. Reaching for their dreams is a quest, and they enjoy chasing the vision they see on the horizon.

When we interview and work with visionary leaders, we have noticed how clearly they can describe the destination. They can even make you feel like they're living it; it's as though it were happening right now. They seem to be able to formulate an ideal picture in their mind of a preferred future state, but the ideal they're trying to reach isn't unrealistic. The picture of this better place, whatever it may be, is grounded, practical, and achievable—but still ambitious and bold. They aren't afraid of thinking big and going all out, but they also balance their ambitions with patience and reason; they know, as we all do, that you can't have everything you want all at once. Before we delve too far into how to develop this quality, let's take a closer look at the primary characteristics of vision itself and how it helps you and your team.

Compelling

Being able to define and describe what success looks like in exceptionally vivid terms is an important characteristic of visionary people. They know how success sounds, how it feels. They help other people taste it. The way they describe their vision appeals to all of the senses, but it is never overly dramatic. Compelling visions are neither overblown fantasies nor are they wishful thinking. A well-articulated vision is grounded firmly in reality and captures the overall purpose of the journey. It reflects the needs of customers, employees, owners, and other stakeholders, but most importantly, the vision differentiates the organization from its rivals. A vision should be visual, memorable, and energizing, providing people with the direction and clarity they crave—and that must be present for the organization to move forward as a strong, cohesive entity.

Simple

Strategic leaders are most successful when they have a vision that is simple, concise, and memorable. Don't overcomplicate it. Think of it as a battle cry or your team's mantra. It should be easy to remember and share with others, and it should answer the question, "Where do we want to go and what do we want to be?" Followers get engaged when leaders provide them with a vivid description, add some color to the picture, give plenty of context, and help them see the opportunities and possibilities. It motivates them to help pull the strategic wagon.

Consistent

One of the most important contributions that a strategic leader can make is providing the team with a stable and consistent vision. This vision should have the ability to unlock the motivation and discretionary performance of their people in a big way and provide a cause for people to rally behind. Without a doubt, there will be times when new opportunities emerge or disruptions occur that require leaders to reassess, adapt to changing conditions, or go after new and better opportunities. But as much as possible, the vision should serve as a guiding light that people can rely on, even in times of turmoil and uncertainty. Only the process by which the vision is achieved is changeable; the vision itself should be consistent over time. When members of the organization buy into the vision, they get excited about the future, which makes the daily grind more bearable and the everyday routine more meaningful. We have found that leaders with vision create greater loyalty, stronger connections, and deeper employee engagement across the organization.

Decision Filter

A clear and compelling vision acts like a filter for the decisions people have to make on an ongoing basis. Each day, people have to decide what to do—and what not to do. We remind many of the leaders we work with that success is achieved by making smart tradeoffs. The vision informs people's behavior and helps them choose how to act and what to do. In sports, they refer to this concept as "chalking the field." Chalking the field lets players know where the lines are and what is out of bounds. Without having some boundaries in place, it is difficult for people to prioritize, see where to aim, and know how to get to where they need to go. A vision does a very similar job by providing a few guidelines that point people in the right direction. When the boundaries, purpose, destination, and larger goals have been communicated clearly, people don't need to be micromanaged and require much less oversight.

Focused

Visionary leaders don't get carried away or try to be all things to all people. By the same token, they don't try to be the best at everything, either. Instead, they focus the bulk of their attention on the things that will make their team and the organization different, unique, or better than the competition in some way. The lesson is this: Be selective. Choose a few things to be great at—the things that will pave your way to long-term, sustainable success. Remind yourself that sometimes, being pretty good at some activities is good enough. This will allow you to concentrate more of your resources on the critical activities and initiatives that will set you apart and help you win.

Intuitive

Your vision for the future should be based on your experience and built around these four components of intuition:

1. The information you have accumulated
2. The firsthand experience you have gained
3. The knowledge you have acquired
4. The conclusions and insights you have formed

Visionary leaders are able to draw on their intuition and the past experiences they've amassed in order to create a clear line of sight to a better place.

Having a clear vision is crucial because everyone on the team can use it as a touchstone for aligning their own vision, goals, and plans with the organization's overarching goals. It is a reference point and acts as a North Star. It helps people navigate through the dark. Please understand that a vision is very different from a road map or an action plan. An action plan is much more detailed and tactical by nature than a vision. If vision is the underlying narrative thread, the action plan is the setting and characters that move the story forward. Both are crucially important, but they are not one and the same.

Too often, people get wrapped up in what a vision is. They get distracted by the terminology and forget why having vision matters. Some leaders even feel that they lack this visionary quality entirely, due mostly to the mystique that surrounds this seemingly elusive trait. Interestingly enough, many leaders actually do have vision—they just may not know it. These leaders are driven to build an organization that is better off than it was before they arrived. The message they send may not be very refined or explicitly communicated, but it's there. All they need is a way to frame it and the courage to talk about it with others. Visionary leaders are able to share their vision with others in a spontaneous and natural way. It doesn't sound forced, rehearsed, or inauthentic because it isn't. They speak straight from the heart.

What Visionary Leaders Do

The first step to become more visionary is to put your vision into words by creating a vision statement. Going through the process forces you to think deeply about the destination you want to reach or the legacy you want to leave. Visionary leaders take an extremely proactive stance. They are fully conscious of their intentions to shape the future, but starting that process is much more art than science. When priming the pump and stimulating your thoughts about the future you desire (and that will take your organization to a better place), you should give some thought to these questions:

1. What is working now, what got us here, and what do we want to keep working toward?
2. What are we trying to do?

3. What do we want to be?
4. What do we represent or stand for?
5. What kind of experience do we want our customers (internal or external) to have?
6. What outcomes do we want to create or achieve?
7. What is the unique or special contribution we can make to this organization?
8. What kind of culture do we want to build for our people?
9. What will make us different from our rivals or competitors?
10. What does greatness look like or feel like in terms of our products, services, owners, or associates?

You really have two choices at this point. You can create what we refer to as a "vision, shared," or you can create a "shared vision." "Vision, shared" is defined by the leader (or a select few individuals) and driven down through the team or organization. This is vision from the top down. "Shared vision," on the other hand, allows a larger number of individuals to share their ideas, resulting in a vision that is shaped by the group. While we acknowledge that it is not always possible, creating a shared vision is the ideal scenario. To begin the vision-building process as a group, the leader simply starts a dialogue. Then, it is up to the members of the team to partici-pate, contribute, collaborate, and truly own a piece of the dream. In our story, Alex initiated the vision-building process by sharing some initial concepts with his team. Then, he brought everyone together to discuss, describe, and support the final outcome. When people are encouraged to offer their input, they feel a greater sense of ownership over the vision, as well as the journey into the future. Together, the group listens carefully, searches for ideas, and seeks out language that fits the culture and speaks to all members of the team or organization. The extraordinary potential and discretionary performance that lies within each member of your team will be unleashed by capturing their hearts and minds through creating a shared vision. In the end, the powerful vision that emerges from the collaboration and dialogue will create the sense of ownership required for the team to work through the obstacles and challenges they will inevitably encounter. Without a doubt, working together on a vision promotes healthy teamwork. Big ideas and big aspirations need the entrepreneurial energy and collective horsepower that only a team of aligned individuals can provide.

Let us offer an easy-to-remember acronym (VISION) that will guide your thought process as you formulate a vision, whether it's for a personal goal, a team project, or your organization at large.

Use this VISION framework (see Table 12.1) to let your thoughts flow as you aim for greatness and excellence with the product or service your organization provides. Trust your intuition to guide you and your team as you explore prospective vision statements and see how they fit. Like a well-tailored suit, a great vision should feel like it was custom-made just for you. Don't be too theoretical with your vision or strive for utter perfection. Just relax. We have never seen a perfect vision statement. It's really easy to second-guess yourself and overthink your ideas, and when this happens an authentic vision rarely emerges. There's too much pressure. All you really need to do is speak from the heart. Your vision will take shape and be further refined with your team over time. We liken it to getting the focus just right when taking a photograph. Having a vision—even if it's imperfect—is the most essential act of leadership; it's what separates leaders from managers. Your vision has to be something that feels right, something you

Table 12.1   VISION Acronym

V	Create a description that is *Visual* and vivid.
I	Make it *Inspirational*, optimistic, and uplifting.
S	Ensure that it is *Sustainable* and stable.
I	Be *Imaginative* and innovative.
O	Collaborate with others and build *Ownership*.
N	Make it *Noteworthy*, memorable, and concise.

believe in, and something that you intentionally and consciously choose to pursue with energy and enthusiasm.

Don't try to work every single detail into your vision statement. Remember that vision isn't about tactics, action plans, or the mission of your business. Your vision may be informed by your mission, but it isn't the same, and it shouldn't be. The vision is a picture of the destination, pure and simple; a portrait of what victory looks like for your organization; the outcomes that are important for you to achieve in order for the business to be successful in the long run. Vision statements look well beyond positioning the organization to achieve superior financial performance. Vision goes much deeper than that. It should reflect people's dreams, the aspirations that motivate and inspire people to act. The vision statement you develop should create a sense of pride, get people fired up, capture their imaginations, and touch their hearts. Do what you can to make it inspiring and uplifting. We continually encounter people who want to be part of something bigger than themselves. They want to be connected to a cause that they can feel good about; something that is sustainable and enduring; something that will offer them security. They want to be valued for their abilities and recognized for their potential. They want to work for visionary leaders who are willing to fight for the future. In turn, they are willing to make investments in the vision rather than focusing only on short-term, bottom-line results. They want long-term, sustained growth and to produce benefits for customers, employees, owners, and the community over the long haul. They want their vision to become reality. They want to make a difference and live their dream. It's within their grasp. It's also within yours. *Go get it.*

13

The Art of Strategic Leadership

The Rest of the Story

"It's not for the faint of heart," Alex said to his team as they looked back over their three-year campaign to reshape the Dallas plant. "Every one of you has invested thousands of hours and untold quantities of emotional and physical energy in this endeavor. But I think we all agree: the results have been worth it." By every measure, Dallas exceeded everyone's expectations: Market share increased, customer loyalty was near 100 percent, the quality and safety programs were working, a money-making recycling system significantly reduced scrap, and attrition improved. Most importantly, profitability, the metric that carried the most weight with headquarters, was way up.

To be fair, Chicago made progress, too, but it seemed that Dallas was outperforming its Midwest counterpart. Sara occasionally passed on reports that her former colleagues in Chicago shared with her, but these were always too general for Alex and the team to draw meaningful conclusions from them. Regardless, the quarterly corporate reports broke the numbers out by region, and Dallas consistently led Chicago in total volume, orders, customer satisfaction, safety, and other critical benchmarks. The strategy Alex and his team had put in place was paying off. And although they knew that there was more untapped potential in Dallas, Alex was sure that Melissa and Victor were taking notice. Three years in, Alex was cautiously optimistic that what Dallas had accomplished would be enough to persuade senior management to make Dallas a permanent part of PSI and invest in expanding the plant. Over time, it had become more commonly known that PSI was planning to keep only one plant. Thus far, however, there had been no official statement about the fates of the two new plants nor the likelihood that only one of them would make the cut, although corporate had always been very supportive of their efforts.

For the past three years, senior management had given Alex and his team leaders the freedom to demonstrate their resolve and potential. They wanted to see what the Dallas leaders were capable of, and they were prepared to be as patient as possible. But everyone knew that the next two years would be different. Melissa and Victor were interested in seeing whether they could raise the plant's level of performance even higher and position it to be the gold standard in the industry. They were acutely aware that state-of-the-art plants play a major role in attracting and retaining customers and winning new business. Composites and polymer-based products play an ever-larger role in manufacturing, and innovative companies are constantly seeking a competitive edge. They want assurance that as their needs becomes increasingly sophisticated, their suppliers will continue to be able to satisfy them.

During Alex's first year in Dallas, Melissa and Victor visited the plant several times, sometimes with little advance warning. Alex could see that they were scrutinizing the leadership team, as well as assessing what was going on at the plant. Three years in, Alex noticed that their focus had shifted: Now they spent their time examining the team's five-year plan and showed curiosity in the initiatives Dallas had devised to bring about improvements across the board. Strategic decisions like automating production, innovative selection, and training to implement cutting-edge manufacturing techniques were all part of the mix. But the real, untold story behind the Dallas transformation was the people, starting with the plant leaders and including the entire staff. Everyone leveraged their unique strengths and worked hard to develop other core competencies to become forward-thinking and proactive. A well-oiled, efficient, productive plant was the result.

On the third anniversary of The Plan, as it had come to be called by everyone, Victor was in Dallas, and more intensely focused than usual. He wanted to get into the details to understand what Dallas had done to differentiate itself from PSI's other regional centers and how they had succeeded in achieving alignment around their strategic plan. On previous visits, he usually allowed Alex to set the agenda, but this time he was driving the dialogue with pointed questions. Alex was happy to lay it all out for his COO. He knew that Melissa and Victor would soon be making decisions affecting the plant's future; this was an opportunity to shine. At his office whiteboard, Alex drew the simple diagram that had come to represent The Plan's four-phase framework. It encapsulated the principles that guided the plant's leaders and kept them on track for the past three years (see Figure 13.1).

"You've got to be kidding me," Victor said. "That's your secret weapon?" Alex smiled and pointed to Quadrant One. Then he explained that for the first year, the team focused primarily on fixing everything that interfered with making progress, laying the groundwork for more dramatic improvements in the future. This was the low-hanging fruit, obvious changes that yielded mainly short-term benefits. When Victor asked Alex for examples, Alex pointed to retention, employee morale, housekeeping and safety lapses, and other process improvements: "Unless we did something about these issues, the team knew we were doomed to fail, so they went right to work on them. The differences were almost immediate and dramatic, and that helped us to sell The Plan's harder-to-grasp, longer-term initiatives."

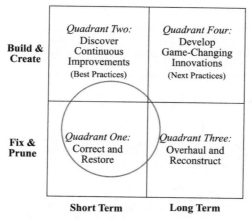

Figure 13.1   Alex's Vision Year 1 Focus

To underscore for Victor that people played as important a role as The Plan, Alex added that it was Mya, with her tenacious nature, who ignited the entire staff's zeal to drive toward meeting their objectives. She also helped the team step back when they met and discussed obstacles and found new ways to move forward. Otherwise, they might have given up or spun their wheels in frustration. In fact, Mya often facilitated the meetings where the team searched for solutions to sticky problems associated with The Plan.

"Okay, I get that," Victor said. "If you're not operating effectively, you can never become strategically effective." Alex replied, "Yes, that's all there was to it, but only for the first 12 months. Then our focus shifted." He drew a second circle in the diagram (see Figure 13.2).

"In year two," he continued, "our priorities shifted to Quadrant Two, where we came up with creative ideas. We focused on basic innovations we could implement to increase value, productivity, and efficiency as quickly as possible. Our strategy focused on adopting best practices and continuous-improvement projects. This stuff was new to many of us, but it didn't cost much, and it didn't take long to get visible results." Alex explained that

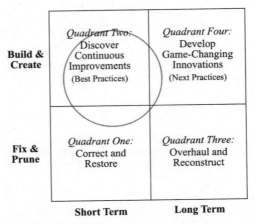

Figure 13.2   Alex's Vision Year 2 Focus

Robert had assumed stewardship of all of these projects and had shown the rest of the team that to get results, we had to understand how the business functions and work across boundaries. Alex went on. "We had to work through our resistance to changing our old ways of doing things. That wasn't easy. There was pushback from nearly every corner of the plant."

"This is where people like Sara really stepped up and made a difference," he added. "Sara is comfortable with change. In fact, she is the one who often challenges the team when they want to lapse back into a comfortable status-quo stance. She is quick to see where changes are feasible. People on the team who've been more skittish about change in the past are now trying to think and act more like Sara. I've noticed that even team members on the front lines are becoming more receptive to all the changes. That's also because we've gotten better at communicating our plans and helping everyone manage the impact. In the first year, it seemed like everyone on the team, except for Sara and Kim, hesitated to move forward whenever we ran into a snag or confronted an opportunity that required a change of direction. Luckily, Kim always stepped up to encourage people who are more cautious by nature to see the benefits of being flexible. I can't tell you how much that has helped us accelerate the process. Everyone seems to understand that there are some simple, everyday strategic moves and ideas that will help the business win."

Victor said, "That's an impressive story. Now tell me about this year." Alex returned to the whiteboard and drew another circle (see Figure 13.3).

"Hmm" was all Victor said, but he continued to gaze intently at the diagram, so Alex jumped in to explain that in the current year, the strategic target or focus was different. In Quadrant Two, it had been about making brand-new, cutting-edge changes to many fundamental activities and processes. They were simply looking for best practices and continuous improvement. But in Quadrant Three, Alex said, "the idea wasn't to just 'restock the shelves,' so to speak;

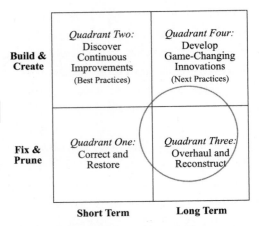

Figure 13.3   Alex's Vision Year 3 Focus

it was to create *new* shelves. It is much more than a 'makeover.' What we've done this year includes developing technology-based virtual prototyping, allowing us to explore new materials and processes and test designs from corporate much faster than has ever been possible before. This is really a game-changing approach that completely differentiates us from other plants. Fundamental changes like these get our customers excited because they hold out the promise of accelerated development of new products at lower cost."

"But Victor, even that's just Quadrant Three. We are now on the verge of the Fourth Quadrant of The Plan. We consider these strategic initiatives as out-of-the-box, original ideas—the *next* practices that will make us unbeatable. People like Jordan and Lu are setting the pace and leading the charge in this Quadrant, but we'll need corporate investment and support to bring these exciting ideas to fruition. These are unproven, cutting-edge ideas, but we've crunched the numbers, and the potential outcomes look very positive. One of the biggest opportunities we see is in new production technology that will dramatically expand our composite-based product line. Our analysis of marketing and sales data, input from customers, and industry projections tells us that demand for these products will reach new highs within three years. Customers want lightweight, durable material for many new applications and products. Our team can help PSI be a dominant player if we move now. And that's just one example. We have two other game-changers on the boards that the team would like to review as soon as possible—ideas that will lower costs and boost productivity."

Now Victor grew animated. "Alex, I'll be back here with Melissa in a matter of weeks. We like your bold ideas, and we have the resources. We need to see a clear business case, so get cracking on putting a formal proposal together before our next visit. You have the space and real estate to do something special. That's what we've been looking for: a team with an exciting vision for sustained growth."

It was the first time Alex had gone into that level of detail about The Plan with anyone outside his Dallas leadership team. Victor had been impressed, and that gave Alex's confidence a boost. He shared the good news with all of the department and group leaders and distributed the work of preparing a solid business case for funding their three big proposals. Their immediate goal, of course, was to solidify the Dallas plant's leadership over Chicago once and for all. After three long years, it was starting to feel like it was finally within reach.

The weeks passed, but Victor didn't come back with Melissa as he had promised. Finally, word came from corporate that Melissa and Victor would soon reveal their plans for the Chicago and Dallas plants. They would visit both sites to announce their decisions in person. When the Dallas team learned that Melissa and Victor's first stop would be Chicago, they disagreed about what the timing signaled for Dallas. Some interpreted it as a sign that Chicago was the plant they would keep, while others argued that Melissa and Victor were saving the best for last.

The uncertainty persisted until Sara got a call from a close friend and confidant at the Chicago plant on the afternoon of

Melissa and Victor's visit. The meeting with Chicago's leadership team was still going on, but one official announcement had been made: Chicago would remain in the PSI family. Sara could hardly believe her ears. She could quote chapter and verse from every performance report that had come out of headquarters for the preceding three years; Dallas's key performance indicators were solid. How could Melissa and Victor have ignored the facts and discounted the heroic efforts and turnaround that had taken place in Dallas?

Unsure of what to do, Sara went to Alex's office and told him what she had learned. He shook his head in disbelief and asked her not to repeat the news to the other team leaders. He wanted time to figure out how to handle the meeting planned for the following morning, when Melissa and Victor were due at the Dallas plant. Why, he wondered to Sara, were they even bothering to fly down? Why not just do a teleconference to tell Dallas they would be offloaded as soon as a new buyer could be found? Maybe they'd offer a consolation prize: some employees might be able to hold on to their jobs. Alex wouldn't be one of them, but at the moment, he was more concerned about his team and how disheartened they would be when they heard the news. Alex knew Chicago had potential and was geographically closer than Dallas to some key accounts. But he couldn't quite fathom how Melissa and Victor had arrived at this decision, especially given the numbers.

Sara later heard that Melissa and Victor spent the rest of the day in closed-door meetings with leaders of the Chicago team. Whatever the meetings were about, Alex again asked her to withhold the information from her colleagues. For Alex, it would mean a long, sleepless night. He couldn't even bring himself to tell Julie, let alone his team. For the rest of the day, his face was a mask of calm, behind which he did his best to hide his deep disappointment.

The next morning, Alex picked Melissa and Victor up at the airport and drove them to the plant. Victor and Melissa made small talk on the drive, and Alex tried his best to join in politely.

He wasn't sure whether they saw through his façade or not. The three of them went directly to the conference room where the entire plant-leadership team was waiting them. As the minutes ticked by, Alex wondered where he had miscalculated and whether he would find words to explain what had gone wrong to the entire staff, who were scheduled to gather on the production floor that afternoon. It felt like the worst day of his life.

Alex fully expected that Victor would deliver the bad tidings, but it was Melissa who stood to thank everyone for their extraordinary efforts over the past three years. Alex thought, *Did she really think they were extraordinary?* Then she continued, "I know you have been waiting and wondering about the fate of your plant. We have some good news and some bad news." Alex thought bitterly, *Are they are going to sugarcoat this whole thing, maybe tell us we're getting a bonus for being good sports and working hard for three long years, then drop the hammer and tell us some other company will want to keep us after buying the plant?* You could have heard a pin drop before Melissa resumed. "The changes here in Dallas have, no doubt, been remarkable. So it may come as a surprise to you that we've decided it's in the best interests of the company to keep the Chicago plant." Everyone was visibly shaken by the news. Then Melissa paused, and announced "But PSI will be keeping your plant as well." Eyes widened, the faces brightened, and Alex started breathing again. "You in Dallas have done an outstanding job, by every measure, of orchestrating and building a plant that is ready and prepared for the future. Right now we need the capacity of both plants to handle large contracts in the PSI pipeline. We love what you have accomplished, right down to the production floor, with your innovative ideas to produce better results today and position Dallas and PSI for long-term, sustained growth."

"We do have one problem," Melissa interjected, and Alex still half-expected her to drop the other shoe. "What we have discovered is that to meet growing demand, we will also need the capacity of the Chicago plant, but over the past three years, performance there has been disappointing. We need help to maximize productivity: fresh leadership and new thinking. Some of Chicago's team leaders will be leaving us; we spent much of our time yesterday working out a transition plan for the plant. We'd like anyone from Dallas to consider stepping in, to repeat in Chicago the miracle you've pulled off here. That plant needs a serious strategic vision. More importantly, it needs leaders who can make it happen. Because you were part of the three-year transformation in Dallas, I don't need to tell you how challenging and rewarding the adventure can be."

There were nods and smiles all around. After a pause, Melissa began speaking once again. "I'm going to share something extremely confidential with you. It may help you decide whether you'd like to take up my offer, but please don't let this information out of the room." She took a deep breath. "PSI is committed to a long-term play in this segment of the market. After Chicago gets to a better place, we anticipate expanding into emerging markets, to buy or build several plants and pattern them after the model you've developed here. That will mean bright career opportunities, and Victor and I would be proud to have any of you join us. Don't answer immediately; this is a challenge that should only be undertaken after reflection. The two of us will stay in Dallas through tomorrow evening, to answer your questions and discuss who's interested in helping us achieve this global vision. Next stop, Chicago. If you're game, let us know. Right now, however, I'd say it's time to celebrate with the entire staff."

The Future Starts Here and Now

What if organizations all over the world were filled with proactive strategic leaders who were busy fulfilling today's expectations while keeping an eye on the future, like the PSI team in our story? If you could uncover and recognize game-changing leadership competencies, like Alex did, just imagine the progress and innovation that would occur. Envision the positive shifts that would take place in the marketplace, on your organization's bottom line, and in your organization's culture. Picture how your team members would be more engaged and aligned around a common purpose. This is our dream. We know it's a big one, but strategic leaders aren't afraid to dream big. And in the end, those aspirations make measurable differences in their teams' and organizations' long-term success.

All along we have maintained that there are a small number of unique qualities that separate strategic leaders from leaders of other types. The strategic class of leaders has a different nature and operates from a different set of core values and priorities. In our work, we see the seven qualities we've detailed in this book in these individuals. You don't need to have all seven to be considered a proactive, forward-looking leader. That seems like a tall order indeed—and to be quite honest, we haven't yet encountered anyone who possesses all seven of these traits. However, we do believe that to make a difference and stand out from the pack, you need to have three or four. We contend that there is far too little strategic thinking and leadership going on in organizations of all types. Furthermore, it is our deep belief that more strategic work needs to be occurring everywhere in organizations—from the top to the bottom and across every team and function. Being strategic doesn't have to be a big, internally branded program or system. It's nice when strategic qualities, thinking, and tools are endorsed and institutionalized in the organization. But it isn't necessary.

We completely acknowledge that it is neither practical nor desirable for people to operate in the strategic space all the time. In fact, most managers spend well under half of their time in the strategic arena. We also know that each job and situation will be different, because the definition of what being strategic means will vary depending on your circumstances and the type of work you do. But regardless of how strategic you should be, you do have

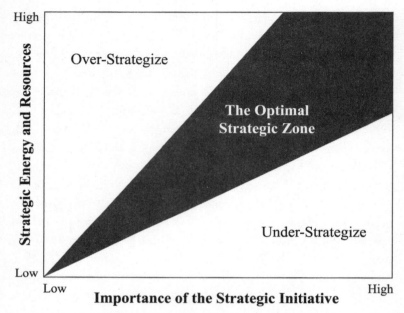

Figure 13.4   Everyday Strategy Is Situational

to have the presence of mind and situational awareness to discern when it is time to unleash your talents, skills, and natural qualities and pay attention to strategic needs—and when you need to focus on routine activities, put out fires, and respond to the crises that befall all of us from time to time. Figure 13.4 illustrates this point.

Because strategy is situational, your optimal strategic zone is something that you need to discover for yourself. The more important or significant the task, the more energy and resources will be required to get into the optimal strategic zone. On the one hand, it's important not to over-strategize to the detriment of achieving short-term results and meeting current expectations. But on the other hand, it's also important not to under-strategize and put your long-term success in jeopardy. As you become more competent as a strategic, forward-looking leader, you will find that these same principles also apply to the daily challenges, situations, projects, or tasks you face. In our work, we call this Everyday Strategy.

We hope that you have now discovered that strategic leadership isn't just another tool in your leadership toolkit—it's how leaders at every level of the business think, feel, and act with strategic intent. It's the heart of modern leadership and what organizations now need and expect from their leaders. Being able to expertly execute on short-term requirements is no longer enough; to be truly successful, leaders must be able to look forward and anticipate the changes coming around the next bend more than ever before. When we spend less time being caught off guard and more time preparing for the future, everyone benefits.

We promise that these principles work. We've seen them in action. They change lives, teams, and organizations. All you have to do is put them into practice and let them grow, just as Alex did. Maybe you have more in common with Jordan or Lu. Maybe you feel more like Sara or Robert. The leadership characteristics you embody might be closer to Kim or Mya. Maybe you feel the most kinship with Alex. Whatever your strengths are, draw on them—and then work on the areas that are your personal opportunities for improvement. That's what it took for the Dallas team to be successful. They all had to leverage their strengths, develop their skills in the areas where they were less strong, and work together as a team with their strategic objective in mind. We hope that this story and the practical ideas woven throughout helped you look at leadership and your responsibilities in a fundamentally different way and, perhaps, that you were able to discover one or two areas to work on as a leader yourself.

Every day, we see people who have either deliberately chosen to be proactive in their approach to their responsibilities or who just naturally function that way. Sometimes it's a personality trait; it's not a conscious choice, they're just wired that way. Each day, these leaders simply show up and contribute a long-term perspective to the organization without giving it a second thought. If you are one of the lucky few who are naturally hardwired to be strategic, this whole discussion may seem like common sense. But for masses of leaders out there, there is a real need to understand, uncover, nurture, and further develop their latent strategic capabilities. To fulfill your responsibilities as a strategic leader—in whatever role you may play in the organization—you need to develop these qualities further. Doing so will allow you to work with intent to unleash the human potential and talent in your organization so you can create the future you want. The first, simple step is changing your mindset. Instead of thinking "Strategy isn't my job," tell yourself, "Strategy is an important part of my job," and believe it. It's the truth.

Now that you've read about these ideas, you may be feeling a newfound sense of commitment and motivation to be a shaper of the future. Take that spark and ignite it—and then continue to stoke the fire. Without nurturing that tiny spark, it's easy to let it fizzle out or be smothered by daily demands. The key to achieving lasting change is simply to get some small, early wins. Start incorporating the principles wherever you can. Don't let yourself get frustrated if you aren't developing the characteristics as fast as you would like or in the way that you want. Strategy-focused leadership is an art. Be patient. Let it grow and evolve. Do whatever you can, whenever you can. Your transformation won't happen overnight, but soon enough, we promise that you will start to feel the satisfaction and see the results that come from being proactive and making a strategic difference. We are dedicated to and passionate about our mission to help leaders discover their strengths and opportunities for improvement. We will be on this journey for many years to come, and as your journey continues to unfold, we invite you to reach out to us and share your thoughts and experiences.

Winston Churchill said, "To every man there comes a moment when he is figuratively tapped on the shoulder and offered a chance to do a special thing, unique to him and fitted to his talent. What a tragedy if that moment finds him unprepared or unqualified for the work which would be his finest hour." You are being tapped on the shoulder. Now is the time to create a strategic masterpiece of your own.

Connect and Continue the Journey

Visit and Comment on CMOE's Blog
http://www.cmoe.com/blog

Connect with CMOE on LinkedIn
http://www.linkedin.com/company/cmoe

Connect with CMOE on Facebook
http://www.facebook.com/CMOEinc

Download CMOE's Express Coaching App
http://goo.g./iI77k

Connect with CMOE on Google+
http://goo.g./BZNmX

Connect with CMOE on Twitter
http://mobile.twitter.com/cmoe

Connect with CMOE on Pinterest
http://pinterest.com/cmoeinc/

Connect and Continue the Journey

About the Authors

D r. Steven J. Stowell and Stephanie S. Mead have over 50 years of combined experience designing and delivering workshops and customized learning experiences for the world's largest companies in more than 30 countries and covering dozens of leadership and management topics. These topics include Applied Strategic Thinking®, Strategic Leadership, Virtual Leadership, Coaching TIPS²™, Coaching Skills, Teamwork, Emotional Intelligence, Communication Skills, Conflict and Collaboration, and Innovation and Change. They co-authored four books related to these topics: *Strategy Is Everyone's Job* (CMOE Press, 2013), *The Team Approach* (CMOE Press, 2nd ed., 2012), *Ahead of the Curve* (CMOE Press, 2005), and *Leading Groups to Solutions* (CMOE Press, 2002).

Steven J. Stowell, Ph.D. is the founder and president of the Center for Management and Organization Effectiveness (CMOE). Founded in 1978, CMOE specializes in management, leadership, and organization development products and services. Steve specializes in facilitating, training, and delivering training to senior and executive leadership teams that help them develop the skills required to transform organizations into high-performance, team-oriented entities, assist leaders to define their strategic direction(s), and improve relationships among teams that face serious challenges and issues. Steve also spends time coaching senior leaders and executives on a one-on-one basis to further develop skills that help them maximize their performance level.

Steve earned his Ph.D. from the University of Utah and served on the faculty at Oklahoma State University and the University of Utah. In addition to the books listed above, he co-authored three other books. *The Coach* (CMOE Press, 1987; 2nd ed. 1998), *TeamWork* (CMOE Press, 1994), and *Win–Win Partnerships* (CMOE Press, 1996). Steve and his wife, Debbie, live in Salt Lake City, Utah and have four children.

Stephanie S. Mead, MBA is the senior vice president of CMOE and spent her career in operations management, leadership development, curriculum design, and organization effectiveness consulting. During her tenure at CMOE, Stephanie built an extensive portfolio of leadership training and development topics. She also worked closely with some of the world's leading organizations to create complete leadership development and training programs. Stephanie earned her MBA and specialty certifications in organization development and human resource management from Westminster College. Stephanie also possesses a BS in management with an emphasis in organization behavior from Brigham Young University. Stephanie lives in Salt Lake City, Utah with her husband, Eric, and their three daughters.

Products and Services Available

The Center for Management and Organization Effectiveness (CMOE) was founded in 1978 with the vision and mission to help organizations improve their leadership and team-member skills through training, consulting, and research services. Over the years, CMOE has developed highly effective, skill-based training programs, workshops, materials, and high-impact experiences that address the specific learning and development needs of individuals and organizations. Our content is designed around timely, applicable research that has practical, easily transferable relevance in the workplace. CMOE also continues to develop customized courses for our clients that make an impact on the leaders and team members of today and tomorrow. In addition, CMOE has certified facilitators located in all regions of the world, making us one of the most flexible service providers in our industry.

Sample Workshops

Applied Strategic Thinking™	Virtual Leadership
Strategic Leadership	Mini-MBA
Coaching Skills	Facilitation Skills
Coaching TIPS²™	Transition into Leadership
Exploring Teamwork	Advanced Management and Leadership
Qualities of Leadership	Custom workshops and curricula

For a complete list of topics, for both standalone and customized workshops, please visit www.CMOE.com.

Delivery Methods

Classroom workshops	Train-the-trainer services
Blended learning	Webinars (live or on-demand)
Individual coaching and mentoring	Webcasts (live or on-demand)
Sustainability services	Offsite retreats

Why CMOE?

- Committed design and facilitation teams with experience in different topics, industries, and countries.
- Unparalleled professionalism and customer service.
- Cost-effective solutions with measurable business results and ROI.
- Research-based organization with practical and transferable solutions.
- Processes for sustaining changes and client partnership over the long term.

Index

Note: Page references in *italics* refer to figures.

A

Abbey, Edward, 81
Accountability, ownership and, 58–59
Action, awareness and, 130
Adversity, coping with, 76–77
Agility, 99–115
  case study example, 101–105
  defined, 105–107
  for dexterity, 108–110
  flexibility and, 114–115
  for growth, 110–111
  for speed, 107–108
  for strategic and operational work, 112–113
Alex (case study). *See* Case study
Atkinson, Tom, 125
Awareness, 117–131

  case study example, 119–123
  defined, 124
  exercising discipline and, 124–126
  gathering information and, 126–128
  importance of, 130–131
  inferring meaning and, 128–129
  for taking intelligent action, 130

B

Bennis, Warren, 3
Best practices (four-phase framework), *170,* 170–171
Brainstorming, 145
Business plan (case study), 11–17
  employees of, 15–17
  globalization and, 14

Business plan (case study),
     (*continued*)
  manufacturing by, 13–14
  merger of, 14–17
  ownership and
     understanding of, 54–56
  products of, 13

C
Case study
  agility example, 101–105
  awareness example,
     119–123
  business plan of, 11–17
  driving change example,
     135–140
  four-phase framework
     ("The Plan"), 167–176,
     169, 170, 172
  leader qualities example,
     19–27
  overview, 9
  ownership example, 47–53
  risk management example,
     81–87
  team, 29–35
  tenacity example, 65–70
  vision example, 151–156
  See also Agility; Awareness;
     Change; Ownership;
     Risk; Strategic leadership;
     Tenacity; Vision
"Chalking the field," 158
Change, 133–148
  case study example,
     135–140
  change-averse individuals,
     142

change-seeking individuals,
     142–143
change-tolerant individuals,
     142
  defined, 140
  fix-and-prune issues (Phase
     Two), 22, 32–36, 43
  implementing, 147–148
  initiating, *26,* 26–27,
     31–35
  for innovation, 145–146
  long-term blueprint (Phase
     Three), 22–23
  observation for (Phase
     One), 22, 33, 35, 37–43,
     41
  perspective on, 141–143
  quest for, 143–144
  resistance to, 146–147
Churchill, Winston, 180
Compelling vision, 157
Consistency, 157–158
Correct and restore
     (four-phase framework),
     169, 169–170

D
Dashboard, for awareness,
     126–128
Davis, Jocelyn R., 125
Decision making, 158
Dexterity, agility and,
     108–110
Discipline, 124–126
Discretionary performance,
     57
Douglas, William O., 96
Drive

for change, 140, 141 (*See also* Change)
for tenacity, 71–74
See also Change
"D's, three" (delete, delegate, defer), 78

E
Edison, Thomas, 73
Enterprise mindset, need for, 33–35
Entrepreneurial spirit, ownership and, 56–58
Environment, awareness of, 128–129

F
Failure, overcoming fear of, 96–97
Fiscal responsibility, ownership and, 60–61
Fix-and-prune issues
four-phase framework (case study), 167–176, *169, 170, 172*
for Phase Two of change, 22, 32–36, 43 (*See also* Change)
See also Case study
Flexibility, agility and, 114–115
Focus
four-phase framework (case study), 167–176, *169, 170, 172*
of visionary leaders, 159
Four-phase framework (case study), 167–176, *169, 170, 172*

G
Gates, Bill, 126
Goals, tenacity and, 75–76
Groupthink, 93
Growth, agility and, 110–111

H
Harvard Business Review, 125

I
Information gathering, 126–128
Innovation, 145–146
Intuition, 159–160

K
Kouzes, James, 3

L
Leader qualities, 19–27
to initiate change, *26,* 26–27
leadership-competency models, 5, 6–9
leadership team characteristics, 24–26, *25*
observation by leaders (Phase One), 22, 33, 35, 37–43, *41*
routines of leaders, 3
styles of leaders, 142–143
transition and, 21–24
See also Strategic leadership
Leadership Challenge, The (Kouzes, Posner), 3
Long-term blueprint (Phase Three, of change), 22–23

M

Meaning, inferring, 128–129

Microsoft, 126

N

Next practices (four-phase framework), 172

O

Observation (Phase One, of change), 22, 33, 35, 37–43, *41*

Openness, 49

Operational issues. *See* Fix-and-prune issues

Optimism, tenacity and, 76

Organizational culture

for driving change, 143–144

ownership and, 53–61

silos in, 32–33, 50, 54

taking risk and, 93–94

Overhaul and construct (four-phase framework), 171–172, *172*

Ownership, 45–61

accountability for, 58–59

benefits of, 61

entrepreneurial spirit and, 56–58

for fiscal responsibility, 60–61

importance of ownership culture, 53–54

overview (case study), 47–53

understanding business for, 54–56

of white space, 59–60

P

Pacing, need for, 77–78

Perseverance, 71, 74–75

Plato, 60

Polymer Solutions, Inc. (PSI). *See* Case study

Posner, Barry, 3

Prioritization, awareness and, 126–128

Proactive leadership, importance of, 4, 5, 6–9. *See also* Strategic leadership

Prudence, as virtue, 60

R

Reflection, need for, 125–126

Risk, 79–97

assumptions about, *90,* 90–91

beliefs and values about, 91–92

case study example, 81–87

defined, 87–88

familiarity and experience with, 93

fear of failure and, 96–97

frame of reference for, 92

good and bad types of, 88–89

group influence on, 93

opportunity and, 41–43

organization control systems and culture, 93–94

patterns and history of success with, 92

smart risks by strategic leaders, 89–90

stepping outside comfort zone and, 94–96

strategy engine and, 41, *41*

Roosevelt, Franklin D., 89

Routines, of leaders, 3

S

Sagan, Carl, 128

Setbacks, coping with, 76–77

Shared vision, 161–162

Silos, organizational culture and, 32–33, 50, 54

Speed, agility and, 107–108

Strategic leadership, 1–10, 165–180

agility for strategic and operational work, 112–113

defined, 4

essential qualities of, 4

importance of, 5–6

leadership-competency models, 5, 6–9

opportunity and risk for, 41–43

overview, 3

ownership and, 53–61

smart risks by strategic leaders, 89–90

strategic initiative importance, 176–180, *178*

strategy, defined, 70–71

strategy engine, 41, *41*

utilizing, 9–10

visionary leaders' actions, 160–163

See also Agility; Awareness; Case study; Change; Ownership; Risk; Tenacity; Vision

Stubbornness, tenacity *versus,* 72–73

Success, celebrating, 77

T

"Taming the beast," 124–126

Team, 29–35

contrasting style of team members, 31

groupthink and taking risks, 93

initiating change with, *26,* 26–27, 31–35

Tenacity, 63–78

case study, 65–70

defined, 70–71

drive for, 71–74

formula for, 75–78

mastering, 78

perseverance for, 71, 74–75

"Think Week," 126

"Three D's" (delete, delegate, defer), 78

Turock, Art, 74–75

V

Vision, 149–163

case study example, 151–156

as compelling, 157

as consistent, 157–158

decision making and, 158

focus for, 159

intuition and, 159–160

Vision, *(continued)*
  overview, 156
  shared vision, 161–162
  as simple, 157
  VISION (Visual,
    Inspirational, Sustainable,
    Imaginative, Ownership,
    Noteworthy), *162*
  visionary leaders' actions,
    160–163

W
Wall of assumption, *90,*
  90–91
White space, ownership of,
  59–60
Why Leaders Can't Lead
  (Bennis), 3

Z
Zunin, Leonard, 95